THE 21ST CENTURY INVESTOR

INVESTING for RETIREMENT

THE 21ST CENTURY INVESTOR

INVESTING *for* RETIREMENT

SOUND STRATEGIES AND EXPERT ADVICE
TO TURN YOUR RETIREMENT DREAMS INTO REALITY

DEIRDRE MARTIN

A Third Millennium Press Book

AVON BOOKS ◆ NEW YORK

AVON BOOKS, INC.
1350 Avenue of the Americas
New York, New York 10019

Copyright © 1998 by Third Millennium Press, Inc.
Front cover illustration by Uniphoto Stock Photography
Visit our website at **http://www.AvonBooks.com**
ISBN: 0-380-79063-7

Library of Congress Cataloging in Publication Data:

Martin, Deirdre.
    The 21st century investor : investing for retirement / by Deirdre
Martin.
        p.   cm.
    Includes index.
    1. Retirement income—United States.   2. Finance, Personal—
United States.   3. Investments—United States   I. Title.
HG179.M3426   1998   98-24545
332.6—dc21   CIP

First Avon Books Trade Paperback Printing: November 1998

AVON TRADEMARK REG. U.S. PAT. OFF. AND IN OTHER COUNTRIES, MARCA
REGISTRADA, HECHO EN U.S.A.

Printed in the U.S.A.

OPM   10   9   8   7   6   5   4   3   2   1

This book is dedicated to my parents,
Bill and Barbara Martin,
who taught me from a very young age
that she who dares, wins.
Without them, writing would
still be my hobby, not my profession.

ACKNOWLEDGMENTS

Thanks to Stephen Pollan and his staff for providing all the support a writer could ever hope for.

Thanks to those old book-writing pros, Mike and Jacquie Powers, for their encouragement.

Thanks to Jane Purcell for keeping me sane.

Most of all, thanks to my husband, Mark Levine, for his keen editorial skills and unwavering love and support.

CONTENTS

1

DEFINING RETIREMENT FOR YOURSELF

Retirement. The word conjures up images of a life of leisure: relaxing in a luxury condo by the ocean, rising early to hit the links, traveling cross-country in an RV taking in the sights. Seventy percent of Americans view retirement as a fundamental part of the American dream—and why shouldn't they? It's the state they've spent their entire working lives striving toward. No time of life is as laden with expectations, no subject more widely discussed, dissected, analyzed.

Need proof? Pay a visit to any bookstore, where volumes on retirement outnumber those on child rearing. Thumb through the latest magazines, where articles on how, why, and when to retire abound. Venture into cyberspace, where like-minded individuals post notes on electronic bulletin boards with names like "Basic Retirement Needs" and "Choosing Your Retirement Location." Turn on the TV, where images of active, silver-haired couples sing the praises of everything from vitamins to investment groups. Retirees have even been the subject of sitcoms (*The Golden Girls*) and films (*Grumpy Old Men*).

Simply put, retirement is a national obsession. That's fascinating, when you consider it's only been a fixture of the American landscape since 1935.

A BRIEF HISTORY OF RETIREMENT

Prior to the Civil War, retirement, at least as we think of it today, didn't exist. Before the 1860s, we were primarily an agricultural nation. Afterward, we began the great leap toward industrialization. While this transformation was wonderful if you happened to be a business owner, it proved considerably less propitious for the average working Joe. Mass production rendered the individual worker invisible, and ultimately dispensable. Work, which had once provided the employee with both an income and an identity, was reduced to a means to an end, providing nothing more than the obligatory paycheck.

By the time the 20th century rolled around, we were a country gripped by the fever of progress, ruthless in our pursuit of whatever would speed advancement and our persecution of whatever would slow it down. Unfortunately, older Americans fell into the latter category. The popular perception was that the older you were, the less efficient a worker you were likely to be (a myth that unfortunately lingers to this day—one that we will explore later). As a result, older workers found themselves squeezed out of the workforce. The repercussions extended far beyond a mere assault on their dignity. One big question loomed in their minds: What were they supposed to live on?

The first attempt at an answer came in 1910, when President William Howard Taft began pushing the idea of pensions. He wasn't doing it because he was lying awake nights worrying about how retirees would eat. Taft, literally our largest president at over three hundred pounds, wasn't familiar with the concept of hunger. Rather, he was concerned with the nation's drive for industrial efficiency. Over the ensuing ten years, roughly two hundred different pension plans were created. By 1920, changes in tax law made pensions appealing not only to retirees but to businesses as well, and some businesses embraced the idea of retirement wholeheartedly. Unfortunately, too few companies were excited by the potential tax breaks: as late as 1932, fewer than 15 percent of workers were covered by a plan.

All that changed with the Depression. Faced with 13 million unhappy, unemployed Americans, FDR had to come up with a way to ensure that the nation's dire economic situation didn't explode into social unrest, a distinct possibility. His solution? Public pensions, which would get older men off the payroll and clear the way for younger men to work.

Thus was born the Social Security Act of 1935, which established retirement age as 65; benefits eventually expanded to include disability, welfare, and health insurance. Factor in the cost-of-living adjustments that were eventually added so benefits could keep pace with inflation, and you can see why the idea of retiring became attractive.

Of course, it didn't hurt that business, government, and the financial services industry all worked overtime to convince the public that retirement was something we all deserved, the reward for a lifetime of toil. Their joint efforts paid off: workers came to view retirement as a hard-earned paradise waiting for them, one in which they, and not "the Man," would be masters of their own fate.

RETIREMENT IN THE 21ST CENTURY

Just as industrialization in the early 20th century precipitated a radical change in the way Americans came to view retirement, today another seismic shift in thinking is transforming our notion of what it means to be retired. The traditional cookie-cutter, one-size-fits-all notion of retirement is disappearing. Replacing it is the exhilarating idea that each of us is responsible for creating his or her own definition of retirement.

In other words, if you want to wave bye-bye to the company when you turn 65 and head down to Florida to tee off, you can plan to make that happen. If you want to leave the workforce at 55 and sail around the world, that's great. But if it makes you happy to stay in your home, work part-time, and spend your weekends working on that romance novel you've been itching to write, that's legit, too. It's all up to you.

This shift is born partly of necessity. Not to sound like the Prophetess of Doom and Gloom, but pundits have been screaming for years that the traditional sources retirees counted on to help fund their retirement—pensions and federal aid—just ain't gonna cut it, and the fact is, they're right. Many of us will probably need to do some kind of work after age 65 to accrue the added income needed to survive financially during those "golden" years.

But more than anything else, this paradigm shift is indicative of the realization that most people enjoy, as well as need to engage in, activities that make them feel useful and challenged—no matter what age they are. Perhaps this is why half of the people between the ages of 55 and 61 and one-fourth of those between the ages of 62 and 64 are both collecting pensions and in the labor force. Early retirement sounds nice, but obviously it is not sufficient either financially or emotionally. This may also account for why, according to a 1993 University of Michigan study, 75 percent of people between the ages of 51 and 61 would prefer a gradual phaseout of work to the traditional stop-dead-in-your-tracks retirement.

Whatever image of retirement appeals to you, know this: You're the one in charge, and your options are endless. You can work part-time at the same job, or use your "retirement" as an opportunity to launch a second career. You can retire fully, even early. You can return to school, become a consultant, volunteer, or train others in your field of expertise. You can even start your own business. According to Jacqueline Powers, author of *How to Start a Retirement Business* (Avon Books, 1996) and *How to Start a Freelance Business* (Avon Books, 1998) who has studied the issue extensively, approximately 24 million Americans have some sort of home-based business. Many of these are part-time or postretirement operations.

Speaking of home, in this new era of retirement it's no longer expected that you will sell your house and light out for sunnier climes. If you wish, you can remain in the house you're living in right now. Or if you'd prefer, you can buy a smaller home, or an apartment, in the same community. Of course, if you'd prefer moving to a different locale, that's okay, too.

Your choices are limited only by your imagination.

WHICH ROAD SHOULD YOU TAKE?

None of this is meant in any way, shape, or form to imply that a traditional retirement, one that entails a full stop of work at age 65, is less than desirable. *Au contraire*; what's wonderful about today's new mindset is that you're the one calling the shots. You decide when and if to stop working. You choose where and how to live. You determine how much and what kind of financial resources you'll need to be able to do it your way.

But in order to make your retirement work for you rather than vice versa, you must know what it is you want, and plan accordingly. Indeed, planning and preparation are crucial. More than 75 percent of retirees who said they were completely prepared characterized their retirement as exciting and fulfilling, according to Jacquie Powers.

So where do you begin?

Well, you've already taken the first and most important step: you've picked up this book. That means you're focused. Next you'll need to take a look at the two major issues influencing what your retirement will look like: employment and housing. These are the subjects of Chapters 2 and 3.

2

TO WORK OR
NOT TO WORK?

In order to plan successfully for retirement, you need to envision how you want your retirement to be. Do you imagine it as the cessation of all work for the pursuit of pure pleasure? Or do you see yourself continuing to work part-time at the job you love, but having the flexibility to take off and travel when wanderlust strikes? Maybe the idea of stopping work in any way, shape, or form is anathema to you. Whatever your dream, the days where there were only two choices available—either working full-time or retiring completely—are gone. A number of other alternatives have sprung up, all of which can help retirees create a lifestyle personally tailored to their needs.

Before we take a close look at these new options, let's explore the idea of traditional retirement and what it has to offer.

TRADITIONAL RETIREMENT

The traditional view of retirement—where you turn 65, take the gold watch, and run to Boca Raton—was based on three assumptions:

Most people don't like their work and can't wait to say "so long" to the boss

While many have attempted to pursue meaningful work, for many others "work" is what the word implies: toil, often devoid of reward apart from the collection of a paycheck every other week. For those people, retirement is the promised land, symbolizing release.

One's skills deteriorate as one ages

There's no denying this can be the case when it comes to jobs involving intense physical labor. (For example, your odds of seeing a 70-year-old construction worker are pretty slim.) But this assumption doesn't hold water when it comes to mental acuity. Studies have shown that age doesn't affect mental capabilities until people are well into their seventies. As for problems with short-term memory, there's a way around them: you can carry a notepad and write everything down, whether it's a lunch date or groceries you need to pick up after work.

Most people find leisure more satisfying than work

While this may be true for some people, it's certainly not true for all. If it were, you wouldn't find so many people choosing to work in retirement, often at full-time jobs.

The bottom line is that these assumptions don't (and probably never did) apply to everyone across the board. That doesn't mean however, that there's anything wrong with wanting or needing to retire fully. Indeed, there are many positives to calling it quits for good, including:

The chance to finally pursue a lifelong dream

Maybe you've always wanted to go to college to obtain a degree in anthropology, or maybe you've spent the past forty years behind a desk when what you really longed for was a full-time job in the great outdoors. No matter what it is that gets your juices flowing, retirement can be the opportune time to pursue it.

The freedom to travel

You've always dreamed of taking an extensive tour of medieval pilgrimage sites in Europe, but you couldn't do it because the company you worked for would never give you more than two weeks off at a time. In full retirement, those days are over. There's only one person deciding how your time will be spent: you.

The time to dedicate yourself to your passions

Gone are the days when you could only squeeze in a hike on weekends, or read up on the Civil War in the few hours you had in the evening before collapsing into bed. In retirement, it's possible to pursue your hobbies whenever you desire.

The opportunity to spend more time with friends and family

I don't know about you, but I'd trade my collection of *Gilligan's Island* memorabilia to be able to spend more time with my friends, many of whom are scattered around the country. And who doesn't yearn to see their children more often, or to be able to bounce their grandchildren on their knee more than once or twice a year at the holidays?

Doubtless you can come up with your own reasons for wanting to retire. But as is the case with any monumental, life-altering decision, there are a number of factors you need to take into account before you start counting the days until you turn 65. Some of the issues you might want to consider include:

The impact full retirement will have on your relationship with your spouse

We've all heard stories of couples whose relationship was great—until one or both of them retired and they found themselves spending twenty-four torturous hours a day together. Simply put, too much togetherness can kill a relationship. And even if your partner isn't retired, you need to think about—and discuss—how she or he feels about your leaving the workforce once and for all. Not all partners see it as a good thing, whether the reasons are financial ("If you don't work, we won't be able to afford two weeks in Tuscany every summer!") or personal ("You're driving me crazy following me around the house all day!").

The impact full retirement might have on your physical and emotional health

There's no denying that work is an integral part of life. So it's no wonder many retirees find the shift from work to complete leisure to be a total shock to the system. In fact, 25 percent of today's retirees say they're unhappy about not working. It's not uncommon for retirees to fall ill within two years of retiring. Nor is depression rare: the void that work once filled in their lives is empty, and they're now forced to face the demons work helped them avoid all those years. No wonder one-third of male retirees return to work, usually in the year after retirement.

The impact full retirement might have on your pocketbook

Generally speaking, once you retire you'll need 60 to 80 percent of your preretirement income to support yourself in the manner to which you're accustomed, assuming you remain where you're living now and inflation remains at historic levels. This range wasn't just pulled out of the air. Financial pundits have been citing these numbers for years, and their beliefs were bolstered most recently in a 1995 study by Georgia State University's Center for Risk Management and Insurance Research, showing that today's retirees will require 70 percent to 85 percent of what they earned before retiring. For most of us, this simply won't be possible unless we change our saving/spending style (something we'll discuss in a later chapter), change our attitudes toward investment risk (another topic we'll cover later on), continue to work at least part-time, relocate, or pursue some combination of the four. This explains why so many full-time retirees sell their homes and head down to the Sun Belt, where the cost of living is often lower.

The reality of having nothing but leisure time

If you're lucky enough to be a curious, fascinating soul with gazillions of interests, then obviously you'll have no problem filling your days in retirement. But what if you're not? What if there are only a few things you enjoy doing, or only one? Don't you think the novelty of being able to read all day long is going to wear off pretty quickly? And then what will you do?

EXAMINING THE REWARDS OF WORK

As mentioned in Chapter 1, most of us need to be involved in activities that engage and challenge us. Give these activities up, and we're likely to lose our mental and physical edge; we begin to get "old."

To avoid this, you need to examine what it is that makes you get up and head out the door in the morning. As someone creating his own definition of retirement, you need to pinpoint what it is about work you find rewarding. Then you need to figure out a way you can maintain those rewards in retirement within a framework that works for you. The rewards might include:

- an income
- the opportunity to learn new things
- the pleasure of being with people whose company you enjoy
- the prestige of being part of a respected enterprise
- the opportunity for travel
- the thrill of performing a task you find challenging
- a benefits package
- the camaraderie that comes from being part of a team

Whatever rewards you find at your job, keep in mind that when I'm talking about working in retirement, I'm not limiting the definition to those activities that yield a paycheck. In the 21st century, "work" will be whatever brings shape and meaning to your life, whether it's tending a lush English garden or trading stocks on Wall Street. When you characterize work in this way, you can see why working in retirement—however you define it—can be a positive thing. You can also see why so many people feel overwhelmed when it comes to pinpointing what they want their retirement to look like. To help you sort through what can be a confusing issue, listed below are some options you might want to consider for retirement.

OPTION 1: HANG ON TO YOUR PRESENT JOB UNTIL AGE 70—OR LATER

If you love what you do, and no one is pushing you out the door or claiming there's some clause in the company charter declaring you've got to call it quits at 65, why leave? Maintaining your present job will give you the satisfaction of remaining vital in a field you love, with some perks thrown in. For one thing, you probably know the industry like the back of your hand, so you won't have to sweat learning the ropes at a new job. Your chances for a better salary than you're making now and benefits package are greater, too, if you don't switch careers and don't run into ageism. (Not surprisingly, as society as a whole gets older, ageism is becoming less prevalent.) In addition, your history with the company may give you leverage to negotiate other options, like flextime or telecommuting.

Dale Connors was able to do so. At 67, after being second-in-command at a not-for-profit agency for thirty years, Dale decided he wanted to keep working but spend less time at the office. He now telecommutes two days a week and goes into the workplace the other three.

There can also be financial advantages to sticking around the workplace. For one thing, if you remain on the job and continue paying into Social Security, you can get an extra retirement credit of up to 3 percent a year until you're 70, when you actually retire. It's anticipated that this credit bonus will be up to 8 percent by the year 2009.

Unfortunately, there are drawbacks to staying on the job as well. The amount of money you can earn at work while still collecting Social Security benefits is limited. Under 1997 rules, if you were under 65 and you earned more than $8,640, your benefits would be reduced by $1 for every $2 you earned over that amount. If you were between 65 and 69 and made over $13,500, your benefits would be cut by $1 for every $3 you earned. If you were over 70 there was no earning limit. By the time you read this, however, the rules may have changed again, so you'll need to check with your local Social Security office for the latest information.

OPTION 2: FLEXTIME

Flextime is exactly what it sounds like: employees are required to work forty hours a week as usual, but they decide what schedule suits them best, whether it's the traditional nine-to-five or working from six A.M. to three P.M. Many people opt to work eight A.M. to six P.M. four days a week, taking either Monday or Friday off. Often the only requirement is that you be present during certain "core hours" decided upon by your company.

One of the good things about flextime is that it allows you to structure your day or week pretty much the way you want, giving you the freedom to pursue other activities at times that are optimum for you. "I'd never be able to baby-sit my grandchildren after school if it weren't for flextime," says Marilyn Berg, 58, a lab technician. "I can be at my daughter's house by three P.M. and ready for the kids when they come through the door at three-thirty."

OPTION 3: TELECOMMUTING

It's expected that by the year 2000 over 20 percent of the workforce will work out of home offices, thanks to such technology as personal computers, modems, fax machines, and telephones. This can be done full-time, or on a part-time basis. The latter arrangement is often referred to as "flexplace": you and your employer agree you'll work a certain number of hours at home, and a certain number of hours in the office.

The advantages to working at home are obvious. In addition to being able to forgo the hell of commuting, you can wear what you want. (I myself live in sweats.) You'll also save bucks on parking, lunches, and clothing. Finally, you're apt to get a lot more done since there may be fewer "social" distractions.

"My productivity has absolutely skyrocketed," says Greg Bartlett, 63, a former full-time city planner who's reduced his workload to part-time, and who works out of his home. "It's amazing the amount of work you can get done if you're left to your own devices."

But beware: some people who work at home wind up feeling extremely isolated. Others find there are even more distractions than there were in the office. If you're not a disciplined person, telecommuting can be a disaster.

OPTION 4: PHASED RETIREMENT AND REHEARSAL FOR RETIREMENT

Let's say you want to keep working at what you're doing, but not at your present pace. It might be worth your while to see if your company offers either phased retirement or rehearsal for retirement. (If they don't, perhaps you could introduce the ideas.)

Phased retirement allows you to gradually reduce the number of hours you work over a two-year period before retiring completely. Ideally the company will continue to provide full benefits during this two-year period. Be aware, however, that reduced hours could result in reduced pension benefits.

Rehearsal for retirement is similar to phased retirement in that it offers a reduction in hours, say from a forty-hour work-week down to a twenty-hour workweek. But unlike phased retirement, it functions as a trial retirement period, after which participants decide whether to continue working reduced hours or to go back to work full-time. The most obvious drawback to this arrangement is reduced pay and possible lowering of benefits during the rehearsal period.

Still, it can be worth a try. Tom Eisen, 71, a vice president of operations for a large chemical manufacturing company, began his phased retirement when he was 69. At present, he's working between fifteen and twenty hours a week, and he anticipates that by the end of the year he'll probably retire fully. "I think I would have gone nuts if I'd gone from working like a maniac to having no work to do at all. This has allowed me to exit gracefully, as it were, and has given me time to make sure my successor knows what's what. I'm fully confident that the transition will go smoothly—which I wouldn't have been if I'd simply retired in the traditional sense."

OPTION 5: PART-TIME WORK

There are legions of retirees who work part-time, as the numbers attest: nearly one-fourth of all full-time workers return to the workplace part-time after "officially" retiring. And over 44 percent of employers now offer part-time positions of all kinds. In fact, the number of part-time jobs has increased 21 percent in the past decade.

Katie Marsden, 66, spent most of her career as a secretary, but after being retired for one year, she found herself getting a little antsy. So she applied for a job at a nearby Wal-Mart, and got it. "Three mornings a week, I work at Wal-Mart as a greeter, welcoming people as they come into the store. The rest of the time I do what I want: lunch with friends, do my needlework, whatever. I like having the extra money coming in, as well as the fact that it gets me out of the house.''

Most part-time work, like full-time work, places the employee on a fixed schedule. But just as there are new full-time options, there are also new part-time options you might want to consider:

Flexweek, flexmonth, or flexyear

This is where your present employer allows you to work a set number of hours per week, month, or year, at your discretion.

Job sharing

You and another worker (perhaps another retiree) split the same job, working in tandem to get the job done.

Not surprisingly, part-time work is among the easiest to find. At present, the hot industries offering decent part-time work include retail trade, services, finance, insurance, and real estate. Other good places to seek part-time work are small companies and not-for-profit agencies, both of which usually offer the advantage of being flexible. And part-time positions within the government are currently expanding. Many people have had success applying for full-time jobs and then offering to job-share with someone else. In addition, it's not unusual for volunteer work to lead to a part-time position.

OPTION 6: TEMP WORK

The fastest growing branch of the labor force, temping is where you work at a specific job for a limited period of time before moving on to another assignment—if you wish. Temp work can be something you do full-time or part-time. Its main appeal seems to be that it offers flexibility and variety. Indeed, 31 percent of those who participated in a 1994 survey sponsored by the National Association of Temping and Staffing Services (NATSS) said they enjoyed the diversity and challenge of tackling different assignments, while the same percentage said they worked as temps because it provided them with the flexibility to pursue other interests.

Richard Stein, 58, has been a temp for two years. Among other things, he's worked as a receptionist for a public television station, a bookkeeper for a restaurant, and a man Friday for a popular sports magazine. "It keeps you from getting bored, I'll tell you that," laughs Stein.

There can be drawbacks, however. The pay is often less than you would earn were you a permanent worker, and may be few or no benefits.

OPTION 7: SWITCH CAREERS

If you're finally ready to go for it and work at the job you've always dreamed of, retirement is the time to do it. Many retirees find themselves working at their second, third, or fourth careers—and loving it. New careers offer the chance to explore something different, to challenge yourself, to fulfill a lifelong dream (bolstered, of course, by your pension or the money you've saved and invested during your previous career).

Janet Holcomb, 57, always wanted to be in talent management, and after retiring from her job as a program director for a major-market radio station, she took her small pension and started Musicians First, culling her clients from the many musicians she'd come to know over the course of her career. "Was I scared? You bet," she admits. "But it was now or never. It's the smartest thing I ever did in my life. I couldn't be happier."

But there can be a downside, and it's better to face the music before you decide to pursue this option rather than after. For one thing, the status you've worked long and hard to achieve at your present job will be gone. You'll be back at square one, and you will have to prove yourself all over again. Not only that, but odds are high that you'll be at the bottom of the ladder salarywise.

However, these risks are well worth it if changing careers is going to keep you from burning out, or getting old and sedentary before your time.

OPTION 8: BECOME A CONSULTANT

You've got expertise in your field—why not capitalize on it? Many companies keep retirees on in an advisory capacity; this gives the retiree flexibility and the company the comfort of knowing they can draw on a wealth of experience and deal with a person who understands how things work and who feels at least a modicum of loyalty as well.

Other companies use consultants on an informal basis, arranging for them to be available "on call." Some bring in retiree consultants for specific periods of time or to work on specific projects.

This has been the experience of Mike Hannon, who spent forty years as a high school administrator before retiring at the age of 67. Hannon, who wished to remain active in education, became a consultant to several different school districts, and he has been called in to offer advice on the start-up of three different new schools in the New York metropolitan area.

"Sometimes my plate is full, sometimes not," he reports. "It's completely up to me how much work I take on. The important thing is that I'm still somehow involved in education. It's something I've always wanted to dedicate my life to no matter what my age."

OPTION 9: VOLUNTEER

Let's be honest: America would probably grind to a halt were it not for volunteers, whose combined efforts amount to the equivalent of 500,000 full-time workers. In addition to the satisfaction that comes with it, and its inherent flexibility, volunteering can also provide a way for you to gain new skills or to test the waters in a field you might be interested in working in somewhere along the line. The most obvious drawback to volunteering is that you don't get paid for it. But for most volunteers, that isn't a deterrent.

Take the case of Angelo Ciccone, who, after laboring for forty-five years as a taxi driver, retired fully at 65 and now spends three afternoons a week as a literacy volunteer. "My parents were immigrants, and I was the first one in my family who was able to read," he explains. "It's important for me to give back to this country in some way, since it's given me so much. I figure being a reading tutor is the best thing I can do, because you can't improve your life or get a better job or anything if you can't read. It's helping other people help themselves."

OPTION 10: START YOUR OWN BUSINESS

Of all the options available, becoming an entrepreneur is probably the one that's most attractive. Not only does it allow you to "follow your bliss" and do something you love, but it also offers the freedom of setting your own hours, going at your own pace, and potentially earning big bucks. Perhaps this is why men aged 62 to 69 years old are more than twice as likely as those aged 25 to 54 to work for themselves. "I'm finally the boss," says Jonathan Davies, 63, who after forty years as a machinist for an aerospace manufacturer recently bought his own submarine sandwich franchise in southern Florida.

The biggest drawback is that you've got to come up with the money to fund your enterprise, and it's not advisable that you tap into your retirement savings and investments to do so. This is a huge topic, one that needs its own book to be fully covered. That's why, if you're seriously considering the entrepreneurial option, I'd suggest you pick up a copy of a good book on the topic. My personal recommendation is *How to Start a Retirement Business,* by Jacqueline Powers (Avon Books,

1996). You might also want to contact SCORE (Service Corps of Retired Executives), which is administered by the U.S. Small Business Administration. SCORE boasts over six hundred branches nationwide and frequently gives seminars and workshops on starting your own business.

OPTION 11: TAKE A SABBATICAL

Feeling burned-out at work but not quite sure whether you're ready to throw in the towel for good? A sabbatical might be the answer. You get to take time off—usually a six- to twelve-week period—and you can do whatever you want with the time, whether it's travel, take a class, or simply recharge your batteries.

"I took two months off to update my computer skills, and it was the smartest thing I ever could have done," says Michelle Godine, 51, a personnel director for a Fortune 500 company. "Before my sabbatical, I felt stupid because there was still so much I didn't know how to do with my computer. Now I look forward to sitting at the terminal. I feel totally empowered."

Many people use a sabbatical as a dress rehearsal for retirement, although it doesn't have to be one. At present, about 14 percent of American firms incorporate regular sabbaticals into their personnel policies, and the number is expected to rise as more companies come to realize the benefits of sabbaticals, not the least of which is a revitalized workforce.

OPTION 12: GO BACK TO SCHOOL

Returning to school for more education no matter what your age is becoming increasingly common. Across the country, more than 1,000 colleges actively encourage people over 65 to take classes, and more than 120 universities have adopted special programs for older learners.

You can return to the classroom to improve on skills you

already have, to learn new ones, or simply to study a subject you've always been interested in but never had the time to pursue. Bill Lentini, 72, spent his working life as a lawyer. But now, in retirement, he's pursuing a bachelor's degree in comparative religion. "It's a subject that's always fascinated me," he confesses. "So I thought, why not? I love being on campus and talking to the young people; they're so interesting, so different than I was at that age. And, of course, I love my classes."

Read through the above list again—but this time with pen in hand, making notes of which options you think might provide you with the same rewards you currently get from your job, or with greater ones. (If you don't get any rewards from your job, consider seeing a professional career counselor to help you determine what your strengths are and find potential avenues to put them to work.)

It's crucial that you're honest with yourself when assessing all possible retirement options. Ask yourself: What times of the day am I most productive/creative/alert? What kind of people do I like to work with? What kind of environment do I crave? What do I see myself doing in ten years, twenty years, thirty years? What gives me the most satisfaction? The more honest you are, the easier it will be to decide what you want your retirement to look like and to take action accordingly.

EARLY RETIREMENT VERSUS LATE RETIREMENT

You also need to give some thought to the timing of your retirement decision. Should you decide to retire early, you'll obviously need a lot more money to support your lifestyle (since you'll be retired longer), and you can expect an unpleasant little slap on the wrist from Social Security for not playing by the rules. If you retire at 62, you'll receive 20 percent less than you would if you were a good boy or girl and retired at age 65. As if the government didn't already bleed us dry as it is, this penalty will be increased when the retirement age is raised to 67 in the year 2003.

So if you intend to retire early and live well, you need to start planning yesterday. If there's one characteristic that successful early retirees share, it's that they started planning for their retirement early in the game (often in their early thirties) and were willing to make enormous sacrifices along the way.

Of course, somewhere along the line you might find yourself facing a dilemma. What if your company offers you a nice, juicy early retirement incentive, complete with enhanced benefits, health insurance, and a lump sum cash benefit? Before you jump at the bait, you need to do the following:

• Find out why the incentive is being offered. Is the company doing badly, or are you or your entire department being targeted? If either is the case, then it makes sense to take the offer, since chances are your job is in danger no matter how you cut it.

• Assess whether you have any choice in the matter. What will happen to your job should you take the offer? Will it be filled or eliminated? If the latter, the odds are high you'll be fired or laid off if you stay. If that's the case, take the money and run.

• Project what your retirement income and expenses will be for the next ten years, twenty years, thirty years. I'll explain how to do this later in the book.

• Ascertain your family's feelings on the matter.

• Compare the package to the retirement benefits you'd receive if you continued working—not the benefits you'd get if you retired tomorrow sans the package.

• Be honest with yourself about how you feel about your job. Does the thought of leaving fill you with joy, or do you dread the prospect of having all that free time to fill?

• Be realistic when it comes to assessing your chances for continued employment within the same field.

• Figure out how long personal financial resources coupled with your severance pay alone could support you. This is important, as it means you'll be able to avoid incurring penalties on early retirement fund withdrawals.

Obviously, the decision to take an early retirement incentive is based on many factors. If you find the pros outweigh the cons, go for it. Similarly, if your intuition tells you your job is probably doomed, take the incentive package.

Thankfully, the benefits of late retirement are more straightforward. The big plus is that you'll need less money to support your lifestyle. But for those who haven't made a conscious decision to plan for retirement, late retirement won't be an option, it will be a necessity. In other words, you'll have no choice but to keep working if along the way you've failed, for whatever reason, to accrue savings.

Whether you decide to retire early, late, or not at all, discuss your options with your family every step of the way. You need to take into account what repercussions your actions will have for them, both emotionally as well as financially. Not only that, but other people are often instrumental in providing insights and solutions we ourselves may not have thought of, or are too close to a situation to see.

SHAPESHIFTING

If there's one concept I hope you grasp from all this, it's that retirement is defined and experienced from within. So what if your brother stopped working at 63, or your best friend intends to keep his corner office until he drops? What matters is what's right for you. If you're having problems disabusing yourself of the notion that "work" comes to a grinding halt at age 65, it might help if you think of your life—and indeed your career—as a journey of discovery, rather than something that's carved in stone. It doesn't matter what jobs you've held; what matters is the talents you have, and how you see yourself.

There's no limit to what you can create for yourself in retirement, as long as you take into account whether or not you're going to work and where you're going to live. That's the subject of Chapter 3.

3

HOME IS WHERE
THE HEART IS

I don't know about you, but when I hear the term "retirees," the image that inevitably springs to mind is that of an active older couple living in a luxury condo somewhere in the South or Southwest, their lives a nonstop cavalcade of leisure activities.

But interestingly enough, most retirees don't fit this profile at all. According to a 1989 study by the American Association of Retired Persons (AARP), 80 percent of retirees choose to remain in the same house. About 15 percent choose to stay in the same area. And only 5 percent wind up moving to a new locale.

Why, then, does the image of the well-rested, fully retired couple predominate? It's the image we've been bombarded with, that's been sold to us for decades.

Why is it sold? Because it benefits lots of people: the financial services industry, the real estate industry, the moving industry, and the furniture industry, to name just a few.

But just because they're selling it doesn't mean you have to buy.

Just as you need to abandon the notion that there's only one way to retire, so too should you let go of the thought that you must move to one of a few areas of the country when you retire. Where you live in retirement is completely up to you, although your decision will be contingent upon a number of factors: your age upon retiring, your financial situation, whether you plan to continue working or not, and how you feel about the community you live in.

It also depends greatly on figuring out which locale—the one you know, or a new one—will best satisfy your needs for friendship, identity, economic security, and health, both mental and physical.

To help you decide whether you should stay or go, let's start by examining your current home, neighborhood, and community.

WHERE YOU ARE NOW

The best way to objectively analyze your current housing situation is by making two lists: possible reasons for staying and possible reasons for leaving. For example, some reasons for not moving might be:

Involvement in the community

You've put your heart and soul into helping turn your synagogue into the best in town, have been a literacy volunteer for ten years, and have always dreamed of running for city council one day. You've built a life for yourself here, and it shows.

Friends

There's nothing like being surrounded by longtime friends, who sometimes wind up being as close as family, if not closer. With roots this deep in the community, it makes sense to stay.

Work

You enjoy everything about your job: the short commute, the generous paycheck, the office camaraderie, the challenges and the creativity inherent to your job. Why not continue when the rewards are so great?

Familiarity

You could drive the route from your house to the Stop & Shop in your sleep. You and Doctor Dan are on a first-name basis. If a stranger stopped you on the street today and asked for directions somewhere, you'd be able to rattle off street names to help him get where he needs to go. You enjoy all the privileges and comforts of being a local, and wouldn't trade them for anything.

Culture

For as long as you can remember, you've held season tickets to the Capitol City Symphony, and enjoy the fact that touring productions of major Broadway shows come to the State Theater throughout the year. These are just a few of the delights you can continue with in retirement, and you'll probably be able to explore even more of what your town has to offer, depending upon what you choose to do.

Diversity

The people in your tai chi class range in age from 20 to 60, the mayor of the town is Hispanic, and one of the most widely attended parades is the one for gay rights. In fact, diversity is one of the main reasons you moved here.

Your home

It took you twenty years, but you finally restored the Victorian scrollwork around your house—which, by the way, you're only a year or two away from owning outright. Your home finally reflects you—of course you're going to stay put!

Family

Your son and his wife are ten minutes away, so you get to spend lots of time together. To see your sister, all you have to do is hop on the highway and drive two exits. Cultivating a close-knit clan is important to you, and one way you've managed to achieve that is by living where you do.

Community resources

You've heard from a coworker about a wonderful activity center for seniors across town that you never knew existed. Many people find, upon exploring, that the town or city they live in provides numerous services for older persons. While you might be too young to need to take advantage of them now, it's good to know they're in place for when and if you require them in the future.

Whatever your reasons for wanting to stay, list them completely. No reason is too small or silly. When you're done, prioritize, arranging the reasons that are most important to you in descending order. If you're married or living with someone, have him or her make a list as well, and then compare notes. This way, each of you will be aware of the other's expectations for retirement, and you can discuss your differences, as well as common ground.

After completing your list of reasons to stay, begin working on the list of the possible reasons to move. Some of those might be:

The need for a change of pace

Maybe you're tired of hustling for a seat on the subway and breathing in bus exhaust as you hurry down crowded city streets. Or maybe you yearn to fall asleep to the sound of traffic rather than the crickets that serenade you from beneath the bedroom window. Whatever your fancy, change can be invigorating.

The desire to live in a more salutary climate

Ask yourself: Do I want to be 65 and still shoveling snow?

To be closer to children and friends

Three years ago your son took a job in Seattle, and since then you've managed to get together only once a year. Or perhaps your best friend left New York and is happily settled in

Arizona, singing the praises of the desert air, which sounds more appealing to you with each passing day. Today, family and friends tend to be scattered around the map. But if you choose, you can bridge the gap by moving closer.

Lifestyle

There used to be a movie theater in town that showed independent flicks, but not anymore. Or you haven't had a decent bagel in years, and you can't remember the last time a decent band came to town to play a concert. Retirement's the perfect time to find the locale that will provide you with all the stimulation you need, be it social, intellectual, or culinary.

To lower your cost of living

You don't have to be Jane Bryant Quinn to figure out that retiring to a condo in Florida is going to be a helluva lot cheaper than remaining in your house on Long Island's North Shore. Across the Sun Belt, the cost of living tends to be cheaper and the taxes lower, allowing retirees to maintain their standard of living with little to no sacrifice. One word to the wise, however: Don't automatically assume that moving somewhere else will allow you to live more cheaply. Before you put the ''For Sale'' sign on your front lawn, do your homework and make sure that the taxes and living expenses of the area you're looking at are indeed cheaper.

Your community is in decline

The brownstones at the end of your street have been broken up into apartments. Every day when you open the paper, your eyes go immediately to the Police Blotter, which is starting to take up more and more space. There are certain areas of town where you're no longer comfortable walking at night. Time to move?

Your current home is simply too big and costly for you to maintain

Your house seemed small when you, your husband, and your four kids were all living there. But now that it's just you, the old man, and Scooby the cat, it feels positively cavernous, and you wonder why you're paying to heat all those empty bedrooms. Moving to a smaller home might help you save on insurance, utilities, maintenance, and so on.

As you did with the first list, put down anything that comes into your head, then prioritize. For example, "neighbors from hell" might figure high on a list of why you might want to move. Again, check with your spouse, reviewing the pros and cons of both staying or moving. Don't dismiss any sentimental feelings you might have about where you currently live. Most of us do have a special attachment our home, whether it's the vegetable garden we so lovingly tend or the breezy, open porch that once played host to hot family political debates on cool summer nights. Remember, there's nothing wrong with wanting to stay right where you are.

SAME DWELLING, SAME TOWN

Let's say you and your spouse have decided you want to keep your house. If you know you can afford to do so, that's great. But what if you're not so sure you can swing it? Well, there are a few options you could consider.

Set up a home-based business

This is a great way to maximize already existing space. In addition, there are numerous tax benefits, including the ability to deduct a portion of your mortgage interest and utility bills.

Share space with family or friends

Why let those empty bedrooms go to waste? You could invite family or friends, who would split costs with you, to move in. They could also provide companionship and help with the housework. While multigenerational living isn't as common as it once was, it does have benefits. I grew up with my grandmother in the house and wouldn't trade the experience for anything. Kids living in an intergenerational household really get to know their elders, and elders feel useful and part of the clan. If you do choose this option, though, make sure you sort out beforehand how much family togetherness you each can handle, as well as developing rules around issues such as privacy.

Turn part of your home into a rental apartment
If you're willing to take on the role of landlord, you can make use of space that already exists, and the rent you receive can help toward any expenses you may have. Just make sure that any modifications you make to your home to accommodate a tenant will indeed pay off in the long run.

If you're serious about staying where you are, you should also do a complete evaluation of all the systems in your house, including the plumbing, heating, and wiring, as well as other areas such as the roof and the condition of the exterior. I'm not going to lie to you: For your house to remain in top condition, you are going to have to shell out money to maintain it. Don't think you can defer it, either. The longer you wait to fix something, the more it will wind up costing you in the end.

• If you haven't done so in the past five years, you're probably going to need to repaint the interior and exterior of your home.

• If your major appliances—washer, dryer, refrigerator, stove—are ten to fifteen years old, you'll probably need new ones soon.

• You can expect some trouble with your roof and gas water heater if they haven't been upgraded for ten to twenty years.

• If your septic system hasn't been touched in twenty years, that may need work as well.

• After thirty years your house will most likely require new circuit breakers, heating fixtures, and garage doors.

• If your house is between thirty and fifty years old, it might soon need new circuit breaker panels, heat and ventilation ducts, and casement, double-hung, and jalousie windows.

• Finally, if your house has hit the fifty year mark, it's likely any system that hasn't yet been upgraded will need to be.

Energy assessment is important as well: to minimize costs, you want your house to be as energy-efficient as possible. Most gas and electric companies provide free home audits on request. See if yours would be willing to do so, and find out what you can do to make sure you're not wasting precious energy.

Reverse mortgages

Retirees can use the equity in their home as means of maintaining it. This is done via an instrument known as the reverse mortgage. Simply put, reverse mortgages allow you to draw on the equity in your home while still living in it. This is done by borrowing against your home with a lender, who in turn will provide you with either a lump sum of money, a monthly check for a specified period of time, or a monthly check for as long as you continue to live there. The mortgage becomes payable in full when you die or if you decide to sell the home. One advantage is that the amount of money you'd owe would never exceed the value of your home or the loan balance, so you wouldn't have to tap any of your other assets to repay the loan.

There are potential downsides to reverse mortgages, however. Not everyone can get this type of mortgage. To be eligible, you and your co-homeowner (usually a spouse) must be at least 62, and your existing mortgage debt must be nonexistent or fairly small. The interest rates on reverse mortgages are higher than those on normal mortgages. And, of course, you won't be able to pass your home on to your heirs.

Other financial options

Other financial instruments you might want to explore if you're determined to stay in your current home include:

Home equity conversion sale plan

This is where you sell or lease your property to an investor (usually at below market rate) but retain the right to continue living on the property as a renter, while the investor pays you a monthly sum for an agreed-upon period of time, while also being responsible for repairs, insurance, taxes, and other expenses.

Homeowner equity line of credit

Offered by most banks and financial institutions, this involves your obtaining a second mortgage in the form of a revolving line of credit. You can draw on the line of credit by using either checks or a credit card. There are a couple of drawbacks. For one thing, the interest rates for this type of loan tend to be variable, and there's often no ceiling on how much the rate can rise over the life of the loan. In addition, the more you draw on the line of credit the less equity you'll have in your home.

Relief programs for older homeowners

Don't be shy about investigating the numerous state and local tax relief programs available to older people, either. These programs are designed to hold costs down for retirees. The most popular of such programs include:

Property tax freeze programs

These insure that older people's property taxes are exempt from yearly increases.

Homestead exemptions

These exempt a part of the assessed value of your home from taxation.

Property tax deferral programs

While these programs put liens on your home, they're designed to allow homeowners to defer payment of their property tax via a loan, which must then be repaid (both principal and interest) when the owner dies or when the property is sold, whichever comes first.

After carefully weighing all the different elements, you might indeed decide that staying in your home is the right choice for you. It was for Bobbie and Henry Betz, who converted a portion of their home to support Bobbie's interior design business. Thanks to Bobbie's continuing income and the deductions they're able to write off as a result of using 30 percent of their home as a business, the Betzes have been able to remain in both the town and the home they've occupied and loved for thirty years.

DIFFERENT DWELLING, SAME TOWN

For many retirees, the perfect solution to the should-I-stay-or-should-I-go dilemma is to do both: move to smaller and/or cheaper housing in the community you've come to love. But before you sell your house and commit yourself to that two-bedroom condo across town, be sure you examine the following issues:

Size

Will you have enough room in a smaller home for all your stuff (the things you don't want to part with), or will you have to put some of it in storage?

Personal space

Is there enough room for you and your spouse to go off and do your own thing in separate parts of the house, or will you be tripping over each other?

Family

Will bringing all the kids in for the holidays be an impossibility? Is there room for one or two weekend guests?

Furniture

Will the huge, carved oak dining room table you inherited from your grandmother fit in a smaller dining room, or will you have to put it in storage and go out and buy new furniture for your new home? How will that affect your retirement savings?

Examining these issues isn't meant to deter you from trading down to a smaller dwelling. But these things are important, and many retirees, in their eagerness to "start a new life," forget to factor them in, especially the emotional issues concerning personal space and family.

Don't forget, you're trying to take a holistic, 21st-century approach to the issue of your retirement, equally weighing all the crucial elements to insure a balanced—and thus happy—outcome.

When Dave Stone and Tom Ruhlmann retired, they knew they wanted to remain in the Bay Area; all their friends were there, and Tom was an active volunteer at the local AIDS hospice. They also knew they'd be financially strapped if they hung on to the turn-of-the-century house they'd restored. As a compromise, they sold the house and moved to a smaller one in a less expensive part of town. They were careful to select one that would still permit them to entertain comfortably (a priority for the couple). Their choice allowed them to remain active in the community they loved, while helping them save considerably on expenses.

There can be, after all, certain financial advantages to selling your home.

Financial advantages to selling

It's no secret that Uncle Sam can be very kind to homeowners who sell. While there are always changes in the tax law, as

I'm writing this book, currently one advantage to selling is the one-time exclusion of up to $500,000 in capital gain on the sale of your primary residence—if you're 55 or older. (Any amount above $500,000 will be taxed as a capital gain). Singles or a married couple filing jointly reap the full $500,000 financial benefit. If you're married and filing separately, the ceiling is up to $250,000 per spouse.

To calculate your potential capital gain for tax purposes:

1. Add together the original cost of your home, the closing costs you incurred, and any money you've spent on permanent improvements. Call this TOTAL A.

2. Then, add together the estimated selling price of your home, selling expenses (broker's fees, etc.), and any expenses you'll incur in fixing up the home for sale, such as painting or cleaning. Call this TOTAL B.

3. Subtract TOTAL A from TOTAL B. The result is your gain.

Housing options

The housing options available to retirees are as varied as retirees themselves. The one that suits you best will depend upon your personal needs, desires, and financial circumstances. Below are a few worth considering.

Buying a new single-family home

By this I don't necessarily mean "new" in the sense of newly built. I mean a dwelling space that's new for you, regardless of the actual age of the house.

There are advantages to moving into a new home. For one thing, you can take advantage of the capital gains exclusion mentioned earlier. Many retirees looking for new homes seek out property they know will be less expensive to maintain because of size or a less exclusive neighborhood.

There can be drawbacks, too. You might not have room for your sizable book collection, or your bedroom might have to double as a study. You'll need to finance the purchase of a new house.

The easiest way is to take the cash earned on the sale of the former residence and use that to pay for a new home. Though most go that route, it may not make the most financial sense.

Obtaining a mortgage, while sometimes time-consuming, could make your financial future a lot sunnier. If you're a savvy or daring enough investor, you might be able to earn more by investing all that cash than you'd spend paying off a mortgage. If you die before paying off the mortgage, your estate can pay it off.

If you opt to obtain a mortgage, start your search for a mortgage lender before you actually commence house hunting. How big a loan you can obtain will be contingent on your income, and how much money you can afford to fork over for a down payment.

Be very clear on what type of loan you want—fixed-rate or adjustable-rate—before applying for a mortgage. Each has advantages as well as disadvantages.

With a *fixed-rate mortgage* (FRM), the most common type, the lender charges the same interest rate over the course of the loan. The advantage is that you'll know right from the start exactly what you'll be paying each month, which can go a long way toward establishing peace of mind in an often unpredictable market. The disadvantage is that the lender usually requires a hefty down payment and charges higher interest rates.

With *adjustable-rate mortgages* (or ARMs), the size of your monthly payment is dictated by the rise and the fall of the market. The points you have to pay up front are often considerably lower than those of fixed-rate mortgages. But if you're someone who sleeps better knowing what your monthly expenses are going to be, ARMs can be anxiety-producing.

Whether you have a fixed-rate or adjustable-rate mortgage, if your taxes and homeowner's insurance are included (or "escrowed in") with your monthly payment of principal and interest, the amount you pay out of pocket will rise if your taxes and insurance premiums rise.

Renting an apartment

Upon the sale of their primary residence, many retirees choose the option of renting an apartment on a trial basis— often as a means of testing to see how well they can adjust to living in a smaller space, or in a particular community.

That's what Lisa and Kent Dubocq did. Enamored with the community where their daughter Susan lived, they decided to rent an apartment there for a year to see if the lifestyle suited them. It did, and they went on to buy a small house on the outskirts of town.

Renting long-term does offer a number of advantages, not the least of which is that you may never have to mow the lawn, trim the bushes, or paint the back bedroom again. But there can be drawbacks, too: your neighbors may be closer or noisier than you'd like, your garden may be reduced to a window box, and you may be subject to arbitrary rent increases.

If you plan on making a rented apartment your retirement home, make sure to find out about the possibility of condo conversion, including maintenance fees, as well as parking privileges, building security, and so on before signing a lease. Also, visit the apartment complex at several different times of the day and evening before moving in, so you have a sense of how the neighborhood changes from day to evening. Will you feel safe walking from the parking lot to the building after dark?

Buying a co-op or condo

Like apartments, co-ops and condominiums offer the opportunity to live maintenance free on a smaller scale. But unlike renting an apartment, buying a co-op or condo means you own the unit you live in.

With *condos,* each unit is owned individually, but there's community ownership of common areas including lawns and recreational facilities. With *co-ops,* you own stock in a corporation that owns both the individual units and the common areas. Your shares in the corporation give you the right to occupy a certain unit, and grant you access to all communal property.

Another major difference between co-ops and condos is the way they're taxed. With condos, each individual owner is responsible for the taxes on his unit, as well as for a proportion of those on the commonly held property. With co-ops, the organization you hold stock in bears all tax responsibility. Condo owners pay separate mortgages, while in a co-op the organization is responsible for financing the whole shebang. Co-op owners are given one vote in the organization for every share they own, whereas condo owners vote on a proportional basis determined by the size of their home unit. Condos tend to be easier to sell, because the unit of ownership is more clearly defined.

When Susan Dwyer, a retired teacher, decided to sell her two-bedroom condo in New York City so she could join friends in California, the unit was quickly snapped up by a newlywed couple who were thrilled about not having to be subjected to a co-op board's rigorous acceptance process.

With both co-ops and condos, real estate taxes and mortgage interest payments are tax deductible.

Buying into a retirement community

The main thing that draws most retirees to retirement communities is the wide variety of recreational activities available, along with the promise of not having to deal with maintenance issues (residents do, however, pay a monthly fee to have this taken care of).

As with any type of housing, carefully weigh the pros and cons before committing yourself to any community, as they can vary greatly in terms of cost and services provided. On the surface, you might think it's great to have your best friends living next door and have a swimming pool at your disposal twenty-four hours a day. But these perks need to be weighed against the very specific rules and regulations of such communities. Also, you should ask yourself how you'll feel living in a community of retirees. It's not uncommon for retirees to begin feeling isolated after they've been living in a retirement community for awhile. "Everyone in my community is Jewish like me, and they're all roughly the same age as me, too," laments Freda Linderman. "Sometimes I feel cut off from different types of people."

There's nothing wrong with choosing to live in a community where the majority of people are like you. Indeed, many retirees find it comforting, as well as conducive to forming friendships. But if diversity is important to you, as well as access to culture, shopping, and so on, make sure the retirement community you're looking into can provide these things before you sign on the dotted line.

Buying into a continuing care community

If you're worried about not being able to take care of yourself as you age, a life care community might be worth investigating. Continuing care communities are those where residents live independently until the time comes when they may require medical or nursing home care.

The obvious prohibitive factor is that they can be brutally expensive, with entrance fees ranging from $20,000 to $300,000. Add to that a monthly fee likely to increase over time, and you can see why it's usually the rich who choose this option. Still, many retirees have been known to take the profit they've made on the sale of their home to pay these fees, which in essence acts as an insurance policy: you pay the fee, the community promises to house you and take care of you for as long as you live.

Despite their high fees, life care communities tend to have waiting lists a mile long. If you're seriously considering one, it's better to get your name on a list as soon as possible.

Christine and Anthony Spozza are only 55 years old, but they're already on the waiting list for a community in Flagstaff, Arizona. "Our motto is better safe than sorry," notes Christine.

"My parents live in a continuing care community, so I know how wonderful they can be. But the competition to get in can be fierce. This gives us the edge."

Before committing yourself to a list, find out whether you'll have a say in how the facility is operated should you decide to join. Check out the facilities, talking not only to staff, but to people who live there. Don't limit your chats to only the healthy folks. Depressing as it may be, talk to some of the more infirm individuals, and try to ascertain the quality of care they're receiving. Find out about trial periods and refund arrangements before making the considerable financial investment required to join.

Buying a mobile home

They're not for everyone, but mobile homes offer an inexpensive, low-maintenance way of living. Most single-wide homes cost only 16 percent of the price of the average single-family home; double-wide homes cost only 27 percent of that price. Today's mobile home owner can choose from a wide variety of floor plans, some offering as many as three bedrooms and two baths.

Most mobile homes sit on individually owned sites. Before investing in a site, make sure local zoning laws permit what you have in mind.

If you're intent on moving into a mobile home park instead, find out if there's an entrance fee, as well as the monthly rental fee. Be sure to ask what the fees cover, and inquire about the rules and regulations of the park before moving in.

To finance a mobile home, you can go the conventional route—obtaining a loan from a bank—but most mobile home dealers arrange finances through what's known as chattel loans, which usually have higher interest rates and shorter repayment periods. Shop around for the best deal, since rates tend to vary.

Will and Patricia Guthrie say they took a lot of ribbing when they opted to sell their cottage and move into a trailer after retirement, but it's a decision they don't regret. "The land was cheap, the trailer was cheap, and we've got more disposable income than we ever could have dreamed of, because very little of it was used to purchase either,'' Will says. ''Best of all, we've got enough room for our grandkids to sleep over whenever they want.''

One caveat: Mobile homes can be tough to resell. While the land it sits on may appreciate considerably in value, the mobile home itself rarely keeps pace with the appreciating values of conventional dwellings. You should also think twice about this housing option if you're retiring to an area prone to tropical storms, tornadoes, or hurricanes.

RELOCATING

While many retirees choose from the above options as a means of enabling them to stay in a community they've grown to love, all of these options can also be explored in a new area should you choose to relocate. As mentioned earlier, most retirees move either in the hopes of stretching their money to maintain their preretirement lifestyle on a lower income, or because they want to live in a place that's a balmy eighty degrees all the time, or both.

But selling your home and moving to a new locale isn't a step to be taken lightly. In addition to thoroughly discussing the ramifications of such a move with your family, you also need to take into account:

Quality-of-life issues

Are you well suited to the climate where you're considering moving? Being trapped inside due to excessive heat can be just as isolating as finding yourself holed up in a warm and cozy home to ward off cold, as Eve and Tom Dennison discovered. "We wish we'd known how brutally hot Key West is during the summer months before we decided to retire down here," he says. "We can barely stand to go outside for more than five minutes at a time from May through August! Our air-conditioning bills are outrageous."

What about the pace of life? Will you be able to get around easily?

Don't be fooled by those brochures claiming that Florida, the Southwest, or California is a temperate paradise. Climate can vary greatly depending upon where you are within the state. Also, make sure you find out what the weather is like year round. Not everybody finds the idea of walking around in shorts on New Year's Day or decorating a palm tree with Christmas lights appealing. Psychologically speaking, many people need to see the seasons change.

Lifestyle

Many retirees underestimate the role family and friends play in their lives. They move away from these support systems, only to find they miss them terribly. Some retirees also make the mistake of assuming that the new place to which they're moving will offer the same social and entertainment activities to which they've become accustomed. Don't. Before you move anywhere, get the lowdown on what's being offered, and compare it to where you're living now. Consider renting in the community before you buy.

Housing and cost of living

If your main motivation for moving is to reduce your cost of living, doesn't it make sense to be sure that your new location will indeed provide the anticipated savings? Talk to real estate agents and the residents themselves to find out the true cost of housing and living expenses.

Finances

A lot of retirees move to states that boast low income taxes, or that don't tax pension income. That sounds ideal—until you complete the picture, and learn that these same states often have high personal property and sales taxes, which can greatly diminish your overall tax savings.

Employment

If you're planning to continue working in retirement, investigate the odds of finding employment in your field in the community to which you're planning to move. Even if you're self-employed, you need to investigate the potential for developing local clients. For example, if you provide entertainment for children's parties and you're looking to move to Delray Beach, Florida, you can kiss your business good-bye.

Quality health care

If you're healthy and young, it's easy to overlook the quality health care factor when considering a move. And yet it's one of the most important considerations of all. No matter where you plan to settle, it's a good idea to check out not only what medical services are currently available, but also those that might be in the planning stages. Family physicians can be immensely helpful when it comes to assessing a potential location's ability to meet your (likely) health needs in the future.

So—are you going to move to a new area code? Stay in your current home? Check out the new condos being put up two towns over? Whichever you choose, never forget that at each step of the process, you're the one in charge. If you're feeling a little lost, or perhaps overwhelmed by all the information being thrown at you, fear not. There won't be a quiz tomorrow, and there are no right or wrong answers. In the next chapter, we examine three couples at different stages of life to see how they're dealing with these very issues in planning for their successful retirements.

4

THREE REAL-LIFE EXAMPLES

In Chapter 2, you were given guidelines to help you decide whether or not you want to work in retirement. In Chapter 3, I detailed the things you need to think about before making a decision to move, or stay put. Now it's time to put what you've learned from both chapters together. To help, let's look at three couples at three different stages of life.

TIM AND SARAH HARPER

Tim Harper met Sarah Danforth when both were undergraduates at Boston College. Tim, who hailed from Haverhill, Massachusetts, was majoring in English, a logical choice for someone with his love for reading and gift for writing. Sarah, raised in Meriden, Connecticut, was studying to get her degree in social work, fulfilling her lifelong dream of being able to help people.

As their senior year commenced, three things became clear: one, they were madly in love and wished to be married after graduation; two, they loved Boston and wanted to remain in the area, especially since Sarah was virtually guaranteed a spot at BC's School of Social Work; and three, Tim's dreams of being a writer/reporter might satisfy him creatively, but financially it was a different story.

Money was very important to Tim. Having grown up living hand to mouth, he was determined that he and Sarah—who would probably never command a huge salary—would not live the same way. After learning that the average starting salary for a reporter was less than $25,000, Tim met with his academic advisor and explored other career options. He eventually decided to go to law school, reasoning that he could always pursue his writing on the side.

Upon graduation, Tim and Sarah married, and both continued their studies. Two years later, Sarah had earned her M.S.W., and had found a full-time job working for Boston's Children's Services. Tim got a job as an associate at a large, prestigious law firm. After three years, he was notified he would be made a partner should he decide to remain in the firm. After discussing the offer with Sarah, he decided to take it. It promised security, a certain prestige, and the opportunity to earn ever bigger bucks as his career progressed.

Tim and Sarah worked hard through their twenties and early thirties, determined to pay off their debts from graduate school and buy a house before settling down to raise a family. Though they enjoyed the good life, frequently dining out and taking advantage of the myriad cultural events Boston has to offer, they didn't go crazy. Unlike many of their peers, they didn't accrue huge credit card debts.

When the time came to purchase a home, they were as painstaking in planning as they'd always been. They sat down and made a list of what was important to them when it came to making the biggest investment of their lives. For Tim, who worked many late hours at the law firm, not having to worry about yard maintenance was a priority. For Sarah, who was certain she wanted one child and maybe two, a house with at least three bedrooms was vital. The third bedroom could also act as a guest bedroom, they reasoned, during the time they had one child. Both agreed they wanted more privacy than an apartment might have to offer. They decided to buy a three-bedroom condo—but where?

They settled on a condo complex in Brookline filled with other young married couples, conveniently located near the "T," Boston's commuter transit system. Sarah got pregnant when they were 35 and she gave birth to a son, Dylan.

That was three years ago. Since that time, Tim has continued to rise in the ranks of his law firm, while Sarah is working part-time, teaching aerobics in the evenings. During the day, she takes care of Dylan. They've already started putting away money for their son's education, and recently they invested in a Volvo.

It's not surprising (given their methodical natures) that they've also started discussing their plans for retirement. Both agree that full retirement is out of the question. Like many people their age, they are obsessed with health issues: they belong to a gym, meditate, and make a special effort to cook with little or no fat. They believe being active, both mentally and physically, is what will keep them young.

Both are also upfront about the rewards that work gives them. Sarah has always found fulfillment in aiding others. For Tim, the satisfaction of an incredible income—along with the honor of contributing to one of the oldest and most respected law firms in Boston—is considerable. But Tim doesn't want to be a lawyer forever; indeed, he'd like to retire early—at age 55— and pursue the dream of being a writer, which he shelved in college. How can they do it?

The Harpers begin by grappling with the emotional issues surrounding Tim's desire to retire early and switch careers. Sarah points out to Tim that if he changes his career, he's risking the status he's attained as a lawyer, and will have to start all over again. After much thought, Tim still thinks it will be worth it. Having written for various law journals over the course of his career and having published the occasional op-ed piece in the local newspaper, Tim is confident that his muse is still with him. He's fairly sure that should he choose to become a freelance writer, he will be able to line up work. Of course, it may be difficult at first until he builds a reputation among various editors. Sarah doesn't have to worry about any of these issues: she wants to resume her career as a social worker.

Since they've decided that Tim will indeed try to retire early, they're focusing on what they'll need to do financially in order to insure that happens. Once Dylan hits school age, two years down the line, Sarah will return to social work full-time. They will continue to put money away for his education, as they have been, but they will also cut back on expenses wherever they can. Rather than continue to lay out yearly health club fees, for instance, they'll make a one-time investment in a cross-country ski machine. They'll take the money they'd been putting aside for a possible second home on Martha's Vineyard and add it to their 401(k)s. Going abroad for vacation every two years, the way they've been doing since they've been together, is out. Instead, they'll plan less extravagant vacations closer to home. They even plan to make the ultimate sacrifice: ordering Chinese takeout once a week rather than twice. With twenty good years still ahead of them in which to save, they're more than confident they'll be able to put aside the funds necessary to achieve Tim's goal.

The next issue they're focusing on is whether they can retire comfortably in Boston, and whether they even want to. While they love the culture this major metropolitan area offers, they also love to hike, bike, and walk in the woods. They'd like to retire to a place that offers both culture and access to unspoiled areas if possible. And they definitely want to be somewhere where they can see the seasons change.

As I've advised in the last chapter, they have made a list of pros and cons to remaining in Boston. Some of the pros include their tight-knit network of friends, Sarah's volunteer work at a women's shelter, and Tim's involvement with legal aid. In addition, they're extremely familiar with the area, and aren't too far from either of their families. Some of the cons they've come up with are the high cost of living in Boston, the fact that their condo will be too big (Dylan will be done with college by that time), and their discomfort at the thought of being older people riding the "T."

Right now they think leaving Boston will be their wisest choice in retirement. Since it is one of the most expensive cities in America, moving elsewhere will help ensure that the money they've been saving will go further.

In addition, Tim's freelance writing business will be home-based, which means his second-career choice is no impediment to deciding where to live. As for Sarah, the sad fact of the matter is that as society continues to deteriorate, the need for social workers will increase. Chances are she won't have a tough time finding a job anywhere.

The Harpers decide that when the time comes, they will retire to a smaller, two-bedroom condo in Bennington, Vermont. Why a condo? Because no matter what his age or occupational status, Tim would rather shove needles in his eyes than mow a lawn. In addition, Bennington is close to both their families by car. And since it is a college town, there's guaranteed to be some culture afoot. Last but not least, they'll get to enjoy the fall foliage, and will be able to take long hikes in the hills outside of town.

MITCH AND SHERYL KAHN

Mitch Kahn and Sheryl Glick met on a blind date when she was 26 and he was 23. At the time, Mitch, who never finished college, was working as a car salesman for a Ford dealership in Ypsilanti, Michigan. Sheryl had just completed her master's degree in environmental planning at the University of Michigan, and was a little gun-shy. Recently divorced after an early, disastrous first marriage, she wasn't even sure she wanted to stay in Michigan, being a native New Yorker. Mitch, on the other hand, hailed from Lansing, Michigan, and had no intention of leaving his beloved Wolverine State until retirement.

Despite Sheryl's initial hesitation, and the heart attack

Mitch's melodramatic mother feigned when she heard her baby boy was involved with an "older woman," they were wed two years later. By then, Sheryl had warmed to the idea of remaining in Ann Arbor. She'd landed a job at the university, and had grown quite fond of the small, eclectic city.

The two were renting an apartment and saving for a down payment on a home when Sheryl unexpectedly got pregnant shortly after their marriage. Despite the university's generous maternity leave policy, finances brought her back to work soon after their son Adam was born. Still, the money they'd socked away for their dream home began to dwindle as they were forced to lay out money for child care and other related expenses.

Luckily, Mitch's mother couldn't bear to see her boy living with his wife and child in a cramped one-bedroom apartment, so she lent them money for the down payment on a home. By the time Adam was six months old, the family had moved to a small house in Whitmore Lake, a suburb of Ann Arbor.

A year and a half after Adam was born, the Kahns had another baby, a girl, whom they named Missy. Both continued to work. When Adam was five, Mitch got a new job as a salesman with Toshinko Camera, which had opened a regional sales office in nearby Brighton. They started saving what they could for their kids' education, but that plan had to be shelved temporarily when the university experienced cutbacks. At age 38, Sheryl found herself laid off. It was nine months before she was able to land her current job as director of development at a small, not-for-profit agency. While she was unemployed, the Kahns were forced to tap into some of the money they'd put aside for college for their kids.

Now, at age 46 and 49 respectively, Mitch and Sheryl are beginning to think about retirement. Mitch has risen up through the ranks of Toshinko Camera to the position of regional sales manager. Sheryl has been at the not-for-profit agency for close to ten years now. As for the kids, Adam recently graduated from Michigan State with a B.S. in electrical engineering, and

Missy is currently a junior at Brandeis, majoring in political science. While the Kahns had saved adequate funds to cover Adam's college costs, Missy's have been another story. Brandeis is a private liberal arts college, and the Kahns have been forced to take out three student loans already to help Missy through school, and they expect to take out another to help pay for her senior year.

Last year Mitch's mother moved to a retirement community in West Palm Beach, and after flying down to see her over Rosh Hashanah, he and Sheryl were impressed with what they saw. The two-bedroom condo she lives in is spanking new. The complex boasts both an indoor and an outdoor pool and is less than ten minutes from a major shopping mall. For once, the woman seems happy.

This lifestyle appeals to the Kahns, who dream of full retirement when Mitch turns 65. Mitch has never particularly enjoyed being in sales, and he doesn't want to stay in his job a day longer than he has to. He also wants to travel before he's too old to enjoy it. He and Sheryl have had very little leisure time together while raising their family. The majority of their time, money, and energy has been focused on the kids. In Mitch's mind, retirement is when they both will finally be masters of their own time.

Sheryl agrees with Mitch, but she's worried about his putting a full stop to work when he turns 65. She's heard stories of men who drop dead shortly after they stop working—when their reason for getting up in the morning is suddenly gone. Mitch assures her that this won't happen to him. For one thing, if he finds himself bored, he's got no problem with the idea of picking up a part-time job somewhere, or even volunteering. He's also toying with the idea of returning to school and completing his degree in finance.

They decided to make a list of pros and cons of moving to a retirement community in Florida, preferably in an area that's expanding, such as Kissimmee–St. Cloud. On their pro list, they cited the following reasons for moving:

• No more bone-chilling Michigan winters.
• The cost of living is much, much lower.
• Mitch can golf twenty-four hours a day if he wants to.
• Most retirement communities offer a wide variety of activities to inhabitants, which is crucial to Sheryl's mental health. (She drives everyone crazy if she's not involved in at least three extracurricular activities.)
• The type of medical care available is geared to older people.
• Some of their friends from temple are contemplating a similar move. In fact, the Kahns and two other couples with whom they are close talk of retiring to the same community at roughly the same time.

On their list of reasons not to move, the Kahns wrote:

• The heat can be overwhelming in the summer. "Do we really want to spend so much of our time going from air-conditioned place to air-conditioned place?"
• How often will the kids visit, once they're established in their own lives? "Are we likely to see them only on holidays?"
• Fear of becoming ossified. "If we're surrounded by other older people only, will we become set in our ways? Is there a chance we could become the stereotypical Florida couple, running into restaurants at four-thirty to catch the early bird special, arriving at the movies forty minutes in advance to grab a good seat?"
• Will there be enough culture in the surrounding area? "Will we be reduced to seeing the touring company of *Cats* when it finally comes to play the retirement community's clubhouse in 2030?"

After prioritizing and scrutinizing both lists, the Kahns think it's pretty clear that the pros of retiring to Florida outweigh the cons. Whether they get old before their time is completely up to them, they've decided. As long as they keep open minds and do what they can to avoid becoming set in their ways, they feel, they won't become dinosaurs.

But they do realize that they'll definitely have to wait until Mitch turns 65 before flying south, no matter how much they might yearn to be in the sunshine right now. By waiting, Mitch will be able to collect his full pension from Toshinko Camera. In addition, Social Security won't be able to penalize him for retiring early. Sheryl too will have accrued a decent pension from the not-for-profit agency, and since she'll be working beyond age 65 (remember, she's older than Mitch), her Social Security will be higher than normal. Since Mitch's projected retirement date is roughly nineteen years down the line, the couple also anticipate that they will have most, if not all, of Missy's student loans paid off, and their mortgage will be virtually paid off as well. Thus, any money they make from the sale of their modest Michigan home can go toward the purchase of a three-bedroom condo—the best way they can think of to ensure there's enough room for Adam, Missy, and their future families ("God willing," says Mother Kahn) to all visit at the same time.

CHUCK AND NORA McGINTY

Chuck McGinty first caught Nora Flanagan's eye when she was working behind the perfume counter at Macy's in New York. Chuck, recently discharged from the Navy, was shopping for a birthday gift for his girlfriend. Before the week was out, the girlfriend was history and Nora was on his arm. The two had a lot in common: both hailed from large, hard-working Irish families living on Long Island, and both loved kids. Within a year the two were married and had settled in Bethpage, on Long Island. Chuck went to work for Grumman Aerospace as a draftsman. Nora opted for the traditional role of homemaker. Nine months to the day after they were wed, Nora gave birth to their first child.

Grumman was very good to Chuck. In addition to providing

him with the traditional turkey at Christmas, the corporation paid for him to attend college in the evenings so he could get his degree in mechanical engineering. Those early years were rough on the young couple. Three nights a week, Chuck went directly from work to school. The children—Maeve, Liam, and baby Patricia—were in bed by the time he got home. The growing family was getting by on one paycheck, but thankfully Nora was a dedicated coupon-clipper and a pro at stretching a pound of meat to last three meals. Eating at Nora's parents' every Sunday after Mass also helped them save.

Chuck and Nora were determined that all their children have the opportunity to go to college. They saved fanatically for their children's education, Chuck going so far as taking a second job for a number of years delivering prescriptions for a drugstore. While many of his peers at Grumman were moving into more exclusive, expensive North Shore neighborhoods, Chuck and Nora decided to stick close to their roots and bought a modest second home in Plainview when Maeve was eleven.

They drilled into their kids' heads the importance of education, promising them that all they had to do was get the grades and they would send them to the college of their choice. It worked: Maeve was accepted into Cornell, earned a degree in French, and now teaches that language to junior high students in Buffalo, New York. She has one child, aged 5. Liam attended NYU and got his degree in communications. He lives in Manhattan, where he works as a publicist for Madison Square Garden. Patricia, who went to college at Notre Dame, lives in Atlanta and earns her living as an accountant.

The McGintys are extremely proud of their successful children. They're also very proud that they were able to help them shoulder the costs of their education. But that has created a problem: Chuck is now 60, and Nora is 57. He would like to retire at age 65, but they've saved virtually no money for retirement. Both he and Nora would like to remain in Plainview, but as cost-of-living expenses there continue to escalate, the odds of their being able to live off Chuck's pension are pretty slim. What should they do?

The first thing the McGintys decide to tackle is the issue of whether or not to remain on Long Island. A few of their friends have moved to Arizona, but that idea doesn't appeal to them in the least. So they each make a list of pros. Chuck's list includes the presence of the extended family, his membership in the Knights of Columbus, and the fact that the house is nearly paid off. Nora's list takes in the fact that two of her sisters are only ten minutes away by car, that Liam is close by in the city, that the house is big enough to accommodate visits from the grandchildren, and, last but not least, that she's finally got the house decorated and painted the way she'd always wanted. All are very strong reasons to stay.

They decide to make a list of the cons of staying put. They come up with: escalating taxes, increasing congestion on the highways and roads, and the changing character of Plainview (there are now parts of town neither feels comfortable walking in). Rationally, they know their money would go much farther if they left Long Island. But both feel, in their gut, that they simply can't leave. They love the Island. All their siblings, cousins, nieces, and nephews are nearby. New York City is a mere commuter train ride away. They've belonged to the same parish for twenty years. The McGintys are going to stay.

But to do it, Chuck is going to have to forgo his dream of full retirement. Instead, he figures he'll get part-time work, either at Grumman or somewhere else. Even so, a quick perusal of their expenses has revealed to the McGintys that money will still be tight. Her children now grown, Nora is thinking it's time to bite the bullet and venture out into the workforce again for the first time in over thirty years. She was a saleswoman once, she reasons. There's no reason why she can't be one again, part-time. They'll see how it goes. If money's still a problem, Chuck accepts that he'll have to continue working full-time. The two have also decided to try to use the equity in their home to help them. Since they'll own the house outright in two years, they're going to investigate reverse mortgages that offer the money back in monthly payments. That should help to ease their financial burden somewhat, an important consideration since they're fairly young and could easily live another twenty to twenty-five years.

The Harpers, Kahns, and McGintys, though at different stages in their lives, are all at the same point in the planning-for-retirement process. They've an idea of both their employment and housing goals, just as you should at this point. Their next step—and yours—is to begin turning dreams into reality. But in order to do that, they've got to figure out how much income they'll need in retirement—which just happens to be the subject of Chapter 5.

5

WHAT WILL
YOU NEED?

As you learned from reading about the three couples in the previous chapter, there are countless considerations that need to be taken into account when planning for retirement. Yet all the planning in the world amounts to zip unless you get down to the nitty-gritty of figuring out what your expenses are likely to be. But before taking up pencil, paper, and calculator, there are a couple of things you need to think about.

LIVING CHEAPER

Most people's cost of living falls in retirement. This can be attributed to:

A reduction in the amount of savings
Simply put, most folks don't need to sock away as much as they did before retirement. Of course, retirees should continue some saving in order to cover rising living costs later in life, such as those associated with health care.

A reduction in the amount of insurance carried
It's not uncommon for retirement to lessen or eliminate the

need for some types of insurance, such as life and disability insurance. However, retirees may need to add other types of insurance coverage, such as Medigap (health insurance that covers the difference between actual medical costs and what Medicare will pay) and long-term care (nursing home and home health care) insurance.

The absence of work-related expenses

For many, retirement means they no longer need to worry about such items as monthly train tickets, business clothing, and other business-related expenses. This can result in incredible savings. Remember that unless you choose to go on working, you probably won't have to pay Social Security taxes, either.

Senior citizen discounts

Hit 65 and you're eligible for travel discounts, reduced rates for cultural events, you name it. Many retirees eschew these ("They make me feel old"), but the advantages are obvious— they can help lower your overall living expenses.

LOCATION, LOCATION, LOCATION

As discussed in depth in Chapter 3, where you decide to live in retirement will have a great impact on how far your money will go. We've already seen how the Kahns' and Harpers' plans for retirement are governed not only by their individual lifestyle choices, but also by their desire to get the biggest bang for their retirement buck. (Hence, the Harpers' decision to leave Boston for Bennington and the Kahns' plans to head south to Florida). Anyone seriously planning for retirement should be considering the issue of residence from a tax standpoint. That is, you should make it your business to research which states impose income tax on your retirement earnings. Don't forget to factor in property taxes as well.

INFLATION, INFLATION, INFLATION

Last but not least, you need to take into account the potential effect that old demon inflation will have on your cash flow. It's one of the more depressing facts of economic life: The higher inflation is, the less purchasing power your money has over time. Economic pundits advise most retirees to expect a long-term inflation rate of 4.5 percent. Of course, the average rate of inflation between now and your retirement could wind up being higher or lower—it's simply not something that can be predicted with 100 percent accuracy. But whichever it is, you can't afford to leave inflation out of your financial calculations for your future.

To help you combat the toll inflation might take on your money, consider the following.

While not immune from declining values, real estate is often a good hedge against inflation, meaning any sensible improvements you make on your home when inflation's up could boost its inherent value even further.

Don't assume that your salary will keep pace with it. Since there's always a lag between rising costs and rising income, do whatever is necessary so your spending reflects increased costs. In other words, budget accordingly.

If you currently hold an adjustable-rate mortgage and the current inflation rate shows no signs of abating, consider switching to a fixed-rate mortgage. While you may not be able to get the greatest rate on the FRM, anything will be better than not knowing how high the rate on your ARM might continue to climb.

During periods of inflation, money set aside in fixed-income securities tends to lose its purchasing power faster than money invested in stocks. (Don't have a breakdown if you don't know what I'm talking about right now. This is dealt with in Chapter 9.)

Rising prices means you need to save more money. Make sure you set aside enough, especially if your ultimate goal is being able to retire fully.

Divest yourself of the fool notion that borrowing during a time of inflation is a good thing to do, since you'll be able to repay your debts with "less money." Are you sure you're going to have "less money" to pay off those debts when the time comes?

Review your renters' or homeowners' insurance limits in times of high inflation. Why? Because many companies don't bother to keep them in line with current costs. (Even those that do may not adjust sufficiently.) Periods of high inflation are also good times to review life insurance coverage, since what was considered adequate fifteen years ago, when you took it out, may no longer be so. At the same time, however, make sure you're not overinsured. As we get older our savings tend to increase and our financial obligations tend to decrease; in other words, you'll need less life insurance for your estate to cover those diminishing obligations.

A couple of other facts to remember: Bonds do poorly during inflation, while hard assets like investment-quality real estate and houses tend to do well. To be on the safe side, consider short-term cash equivalent investments whose interest rates tend to rise with inflation. (Again, don't reach for an aspirin if all this financial talk is going over your head. By the time you're done with Chapter 9, you'll know exactly what I'm talking about.) Once interest rates get high, lock in attractive yields by purchasing longer-term bonds. Cover yourself by staggering the maturities on fixed-income investments.

Those planning full retirement should not only put a portion of their personal retirement funds in investments, they should also save some of their income for their ripe old age so they'll be able to meet ever rising costs of living. Inflation is the bane of retirees whose income is partially or wholly fixed, since most pensions and securities don't keep pace with inflation the way Social Security does.

ESTIMATION, ESTIMATION, ESTIMATION

We've touched on location. We've dealt with inflation. Now it's time to indulge in a little estimation—namely, coming up with a rough estimate of what your living expenses will be in retirement. If you're like most people, the mere thought of having to crunch numbers is sending shivers down your spine. But don't be afraid. Throughout this book, I'll be using clear, simple formulas so that even those of you who are mathematically challenged will be able to calculate correctly.

After years of study and research, the consensus among most financial planners and personal finance experts is that the best way to figure out the income needed to cover your retirement living expenses is to follow this simple formula:

> The annual income needed (in current dollars) to maintain your standard of living during retirement = 75 percent of your current gross annual income less the amount of your annual savings.

For example: if your current income is $75,000 a year and you save $10,000, that means you spend $65,000. So to calculate the annual income you'll need to maintain your current standard of living in retirement, multiply $65,000 by .75. The number you'll come up with is $48,750.

But keep in mind that individual plans and financial situations differ greatly. Depending on where you are and what you want, you might need more—or less—than 75 percent of what you're making now. For instance, if you're not making a living wage today, 75 percent of your current "coolie wages" won't be sufficient when you're retired. That's why I suggest you start with the 75 percent formula, but verify it by digging a bit deeper into your financial life. (We'll start digging in a couple of pages, but for the moment, let's get back to our 75 percent formula.)

FORECASTING INCOME NEED

The following exercise will help you establish a rough idea of the amount of money you'll need yearly to continue living in the style to which you're accustomed:

1. Write down your current gross annual income; this should include income from all sources.
2. Subtract your annual savings, including contributions to retirement plans.
3. Write down the subtotal—that is the amount you currently spend.
4. Multiply that number by 75 percent—in current dollars, that's how much you'll need annually to live in retirement.
5. To factor in inflation, count how many years you have until retirement, and, using the table below, find the inflation factor.
6. Multiply the current annual spending figure you came up with by the inflation factor (for example: $48,750 x 1.2 = $58,500).
7. This will give you the annual amount you'll need to live on in retirement in future dollars.

INFLATION FACTORS

Years until retirement	Factor
5	1.2
10	1.6
15	1.9
20	2.4
25	3.0
30	3.7
35	4.7
40	5.8

To give you a better example of how this works, let's take our three couples through the process of forecasting income need, starting with the Harpers.

Right now, the Harpers' combined annual income is

$135,000. Of that, they save $10,000 (Sarah's earnings from teaching aerobics part-time) annually. Their subtotal, then, or the amount they currently spend per year, is $125,000. To figure out what they'll need annually in retirement in today's dollars, they multiply $125,000 by .75 to get $93,750. To factor in inflation, they consult the table. Since Tim is now 38 and plans on retiring early, at age 55, he's seventeen years away from retiring. According to the table, they should use an inflation factor somewhere between 1.9 and 2.4, say 2.1. Their need of $93,750 in current dollars, multiplied by 2.1, equals $196,875. That's how much the Harpers will need in future dollars.

The Kahns are starting with a slightly lower annual income: $100,000. Unfortunately, they are not saving, so there's no figure to subtract from their annual income. Their spending is $100,000 per year. Multiplying by .75, the Kahns figure they'll need $75,000 a year in today's dollars to live comfortably in retirement. With about nineteen years to go before Mitch plans to fully retire at 65, the Kahns look at the inflation factor table and estimate their factor to be 2.3. Multiplying $75,000 by 2.3, they realize that they'll most likely need $172,500 per year in retirement to live in the manner to which they're accustomed.

As for the McGintys, Chuck is pulling down about $60,000 a year. Like the Kahns, they aren't saving, so the amount they currently spend annually is $60,000 as well. Multiplying their annual income by .75, the McGintys see that they'll need $45,000 annually in today's dollars to be able to retire comfortably. Since Chuck is aiming to retire in five years, their inflation factor, according to the table, is 1.2. Do the math, and you'll see the McGintys will need a minimum of $54,000 a year to really be able to retire while still keeping pace with inflation.

SUMMARIZING CURRENT EXPENSES

As I noted earlier, in order to make your estimates more reliable it's necessary to dig a little bit deeper into your financial life. First, you need to list your specific current living expenses.

Some expenses, like rent or mortgage payments, are monthly. Others, like income taxes, are yearly. For uniformity's sake, it helps to take all your expenses and figure them out both monthly and yearly. To obtain the monthly equivalent of an annual expense, divide it by 12. Similarly, to figure out the annual equivalent of a monthly expense, multiply it by 12.

Tackle fixed expenses first. Use the worksheet to list what you currently spend monthly and yearly.

Current Fixed Expenses Worksheet

	Monthly	Yearly
Rent/mortgage		
Loan payments		
Income taxes		
Heating		
Utilities		
Telephone		
Water		
Homeowners' insurance		
Property taxes		
Auto insurance		
Medical/dental insurance		
Life and other insurance		
Subtotals		

Next, write down your current discretionary (and semidiscretionary) expenses, both monthly and yearly.

Current Discretionary Expenses Worksheet

	Monthly	Yearly
Food		
Clothing		
Transportation		
Medical care and prescription drugs		
Personal care, including haircuts, massages, makeup, etc.		

	Monthly	*Yearly*
Household maintenance	_____	_____
Furniture and equipment	_____	_____
Education	_____	_____
Entertainment	_____	_____
Travel	_____	_____
Hobbies	_____	_____
Gifts	_____	_____
Contributions and donations	_____	_____

Tally up your subtotals. You should now know what you currently spend both monthly and yearly, which is good. But you also need to estimate what you're going to be spending in retirement.

ESTIMATING RETIREMENT EXPENSES

Go through the two lists again, calculating what you'll probably spend on these items, both monthly and yearly, in retirement.

For example, let's say you currently spend $1,000 a month on your mortgage, but plan on moving to Florida, where you expect your mortgage payments to be cut in half. Under monthly future expenses for your mortgage, you would write $500. In order to come up with a yearly total just multiply $500 by 12 for an annual expense of $6,000.

Remember, these numbers are only estimates, and every individual going through this process will come up with different figures. If you're not sure yet if you're going to be moving, or what a particular expense might be, but you're pretty certain it will be lower, simply take the current number for that item and multiply by .75. Thus, if you're currently spending $1,000 a year to put gas in your car, but you're not sure how much less you'll be driving in retirement, hedge your bet and multiply the $1,000 by .75, and assume your transportation expenses will drop to $750 per year in retirement.

Just be sure you also take into account potential increases in expenses. For instance, many people end up spending more money on entertainment and hobbies in retirement than they did when they were working and had less free time.

Tally up your monthly and yearly estimated expenses. Remember, these are figured in current dollars. To be safe you need to take inflation into account. That means multiplying your numbers by the same inflation factor you used for your earlier calculation.

Let's say that according to your calculations, you'll be spending $6,000 a year in retirement on your mortgage. That's in current dollars. But you're not planning to retire for twenty more years. Checking the inflation factor table, you see that the inflation factor for twenty years is 2.4. You multiply $6,000 by 2.4, and what do you get? In future dollars, you'll probably be spending $14,400 a year in mortgage payments.

Tackle your fixed expenses first again, this time writing down what you estimate you'll be spending monthly and yearly in both current and future dollars.

Estimated Fixed Expenses Worksheet

	Monthly current $$	Monthly future $$	Yearly current $$	Yearly future $$
Rent/mortgage				
Loan payments				
Income taxes				
Heating				
Utilities				
Telephone				
Water				
Homeowners' insurance				
Property taxes				
Auto insurance				
Medical/dental insurance				
Life and other insurance				
Subtotals				

Next estimate your discretionary (and semidiscretionary) monthly and yearly expenses, in both current and future dollars.

Estimated Discretionary Expenses Worksheet

	Monthly current $	Monthly future $	Yearly current $	Yearly future $
Food				
Clothing				
Transportation				
Medical care and prescription drugs				
Personal care, including haircuts, massages, makeup, etc.				
Household maintenance				
Furniture and equipment				
Education				
Entertainment				
Travel				
Hobbies				
Gifts				
Contributions and donations				
Subtotals				

Combine the subtotals appearing here and on page 65 to get overall current and future totals that include both fixed and discretionary expenses.

Tempted to throw the calculator (and this book) out the window and run screaming into the night? Please don't. Avoiding these issues won't make them go away. Perhaps seeing where our friends are with their estimates can clear things up a bit.

THE HARPERS

Let's take the Harpers through the process of calculating current expenses, retirement expenses in current dollars, and retirement expenses with inflation factored in.

At present, Tim and Sarah pay about $40,000 a year in income taxes. But they expect their move to Bennington will cut that in half, since Tim's income will be dropping dramatically. Thus their estimated income tax payment at the time of Tim's retirement will be $20,000. In future dollars (the Harpers' inflation factor is 2.1), it might be somewhere around $42,000.

As for their mortgage, right now they're paying $1,000 a month. In retirement, they expect that number to be just about the same, since they'll be buying a new condo. Factoring in inflation, they'll probably be paying somewhere around $2,100 a month.

Heating is easy to calculate monthly as well. Right now, it costs $150 a month to keep Tim, Sarah, and baby Dylan toasty warm. Since the move they plan to make is to another New England state, they'll still have winters to worry about. Tim and Sarah therefore estimate that their monthly heating bills will be the same upon retirement. But in terms of future dollars, that $150 comes out to $315 a month.

Similarly, they don't anticipate the $30 a month they pay in utilities to change in retirement, either. But using their inflation factor of 2.1 they guesstimate that the cost seventeen years from now will most likely be $63.

Also unchanging, they imagine, will be their water bill. Right now, they're paying $120 a year, which is what they expect to pay in retirement, too. But inflation will most likely jack the annual price up to $252.

One expense they expect will rise in retirement is their telephone bill. Right now, they're spending about $100 a month, but by the time they retire, Dylan will be grown and no doubt living elsewhere, and they'll want to stay in touch. They'll also be leaving many good friends behind in Boston. For those reasons, the Harpers estimate that their monthly bill will rise to $200 a month. With inflation, it'll be $420 a month.

They do expect their property taxes to drop, however, since bucolic Bennington is a far cry from *très* expensive Boston. Right now, they pay $4,000 a year. That number should go down to $3,000 in retirement (Bennington is less expensive than Boston but it's still pretty pricey). Multiplying that by 2.1, they envision property taxes of $6,300 annually.

Tim and Sarah are lucky in that they don't have to pay anything right now for medical and dental insurance (Tim's employer picks up the tab, leaving the Harpers to pay only the deductible), and (keeping their fingers crossed) they don't expect anything to change in retirement. While they're currently insured through Tim's job, when they move to Bennington they will simply switch to Sarah's insurance (again, chances are they will be responsible only for insurance deductibles). Still, they're keeping their fingers crossed and hoping conservative estimates in other areas will give them enough of a cushion should these health insurance plans fall through.

Since they'll probably be buying a similar-sized home, they figure their homeowners' insurance will still be the same $1,000 they pay now, but with inflation it will climb to $2,100.

Both their life insurance policies have fixed premiums totaling $600. So, even with inflation, they'll be the same.

Their auto insurance will probably drop, as it tends to do when one leaves a major metropolitan area where people drive like lunatics and there are lots of auto thefts. Right now, they're paying about $2,000 a year to insure their Volvo. In retirement, they expect that to drop to $1,000. Taking inflation into account, the more likely number is $2,100 annually.

Another item likely to drop is their monthly food expenses. Think about it: there will only be the two of them. So while they currently spend about $300 a month on sustenance, upon retirement that figure will probably dip down to $200, or $420 in future dollars.

Unfortunately, there's one expense that's likely to rise in

retirement, and that's furnishings. The Harpers' home is completely furnished at present, so they're not paying out anything for that. But when they retire, Tim will need a computer, modem, CD-ROM drive, and fax, as well as a desk, chair, and so on to do his freelancing from home. That first year they retire, they expect to have to lay out around $8,000, or—pass the smelling salts—$16,800 in future dollars.

However, one advantage of working from home is that you can live in sweats, so the $6,000 the Harpers currently spend to look professional will drop down to $3,000 as Sarah will be the only one buying "work" clothes. With inflation, though, the number will more likely be about $6,300.

Another expense dropping significantly will be transportation. At the moment, the Harpers spend about $2,500 a year on gas and on passes for the "T." Since they'll no longer be riding the "T" when they move to Vermont, but will still be driving, the amount they spend annually will probably go down to $1,500 annually—or $3,150 in inflated dollars.

Not surprisingly, two areas in which they anticipate their expenses to rise in retirement are travel and medical/drugs. Since they expect to do more leisure traveling in retirement, the $2,000 they now spend annually will probably rise to $4,000, or $8,400 with inflation. Similarly, though they're only now paying $100 (their deductible) a year for medical care and prescriptions under Tim's insurance, once they switch to Sarah's they anticipate a higher deductible of $500 a year. In future dollars, that will be $1,050.

Expenses in personal care should drop for them, however, as will expenses in education. The Harpers currently stash away $7,000 a year for Dylan's college education. By the time they retire, they don't imagine they'll have any education expenses to worry about at all. As far as present personal care goes, both Tim and Sarah get their hair cut at least once a month, which costs $60 each. In retirement, Tim intends to forgo the high-power hairstylists and frequent the local barber shop, resulting in a reduced expense of $40 a month, or $84 in future terms.

In retirement, Sarah Harper has no intention of reducing the amount she gives to charity. Each year, she gives $500 to Planned Parenthood and National Public Radio and will continue to do so. In future dollars, this means the Harpers will be giving $1,050 in charitable contributions. This irks Tim somewhat, as he tends to be a little less altruistic, but when Sarah points out to him that the $2,000 they currently spend annually in gifts will be reduced to $1,000 (after all, Dylan will be grown and the older one gets, the less birthdays matter), he calms down a bit—even if the dollar figure when you factor in inflation is $2,100.

Both Tim and Sarah expect that what they currently spend a year on entertainment and hobbies will stay the same. This year, the Harpers will spend $3,000 on entertainment. In future dollars, that's $6,300. Similarly, the $2,000 they now spend each year on books, videos, and CDs isn't likely to decrease, culture vultures that they are. But in future dollars that $2,000 turns into $4,200.

THE KAHNS

We know from our previous calculations that the Kahns are dealing with an inflation factor of 2.3. Therefore, while the $30,000 they pay annually in income tax is likely to be cut in half to $15,000 when they move to sunny Florida, in future *dinero* the number is more likely to be $34,500.

Their mortgage payments are going to drop, too. Right now they're paying $750 a month. Once they move to Coconut Cove Retirement Village, their mortgage will go down to $500 a month. Multiply that by 2.3 and you'll see that Mitch and Sheryl will probably be paying around $1,150 a month.

That's okay, says Mitch, because the $200 a month they now pay to keep warm during those long Michigan winters will be gone, gone, gone. No more heating bills to worry about. (Sheryl warns him not to forget about air conditioning bills, however.) Equally pleasing is that the water and phone bills are likely to stay the same. Right now, the Kahns pay $120 a year for water. In future dollars, that's $276 a year. Not bad. Similarly, their phone bills hover somewhere around $150 a month, no shock when you consider that most of Sheryl's family is in New York and both kids have been away at school. That number will remain the same, although after inflation it'll be $345 a month.

Loan payments for Missy's education are killing the Kahns right now, but nineteen years down the line when Mitch waves bye-bye to Toshinko, they expect all the loans to be paid off. That helps them breathe easier when they think about retirement, as does the fact that they now spend nothing for medical/ dental and won't have to in Florida, either, assuming Toshinko and Medicare don't go bust. Also delightful is that their property taxes are likely to plummet, too. The $2,000 they now spend annually will go down to $750, or $1,725 in future dollars.

When it comes to insurance, their auto and homeowners' insurance premiums are likely to drop, but their life insurance costs will probably rise. Currently they pay $1,000 a year to insure their car. In Florida, even with all those drivers who can barely see over the dashboard, the number will probably drop to $500, or $1,150 if you multiply that figure by 2.3. Homeowners' insurance will drop $200 a year from $500 to $300. However, the possibility that inflation will push it up to $690 is strong.

As for life insurance, the $300 they're spending annually will rise to $600 by the time they retire (no one ever said it was fun getting older, folks), or $1,380 in future dollars. By the way, this increase isn't due to their taking out more insurance. It's just that the premiums on their term policies will go up.

Since they expect to eat out more when they retire, the Kahns imagine that their grocery bills will shrink while their entertainment expenses rise. Hence, the $200 a month they now spend at the supermarket will most likely go down to $150 (or $345, factoring in inflation), but the $200 a month they now spend on dining out and seeing movies will probably go up to $400, or a shocking $920 a month if multiplied by the 2.3 inflation factor.

Also rising will be their furnishing expenses. Their present home, like the Harpers', is completely furnished. But when they move, they plan on selling their furniture and buying all new stuff for their condo's two bedrooms, living room, and kitchen. They estimate they'll spend $10,000 doing so, which works out to $23,000 in future dollars.

Three areas where their expenses are likely to remain the same are transportation, medical/drugs, and personal care. Right now, it costs the Kahns about $83 a month to gas up their car. This, they believe, will be the same in retirement, except in future dollars the cost will be $191 a month. Under their medical insurance plan, the Kahns have a $500-a-year deductible, and they expect to carry that through retirement. The result in future dollars: $1,150 a year.

As for personal care, both Mitch and Sheryl now get their hair cut once a month, and Sheryl makes a weekly trip to the nail salon. The monthly cost is $210, and since they plan on maintaining the same grooming routine, that's what it'll be in retirement, too—except in future dollars the monthly expense will be around $483 a month.

One area of expense that will change dramatically for the Kahns in retirement is what they spend on education. The sum they have been spending per month is $500, thanks to Adam and Missy and (as Mother Kahn calls them) "their fancy schmancy schools." But by the time they retire, the Kahns imagine (*pray* is probably a better word) that expenses for their children's education will be at an end.

Another area that will see a dramatic decrease is travel. The Kahns rack up lots of frequent flyer miles; what with having to visit Mother Kahn in Florida, Sheryl's family in New York, and the kids at school, it has been costing them about $5,000. However, once they move to Florida, they intend to stay put, and only venture off to see their children. ("Let people come see us," they reason.) Thus the amount they expect to spend annually in travel drops to $1,000—or $2,300 if you count inflation.

Also dropping will be the amount they spend in contributions. Right now the Kahns donate about $1,000 a year to their temple. But all that's going to change once they move to Florida, claims Mitch, who says he'll be damned if he'll give more than $500 a year just to ensure a seat on the high holy days. If Mitch sticks to his word, the Kahns will be giving their new congregation $1,150 a year in future dollars.

Remaining the same in retirement is the amount the Kahns spend on gifts. Right now, it's about $1,200 a year, what with birthdays and Hanukkah. "What could change?" Sheryl asks. Nothing. Except that in future dollars, that figure is $2,760.

Last but not least, the Kahns know that the Mitch's addiction to golf is going to cost them when they head south. He spends about $1,800 a year on golf goodies and fees, and he has no intention of denying himself anything when he gets to Florida. That will drive the number up to $3,600 annually, or a frightening $8,280 after inflation. As for Sheryl, her hobbies—water aerobics and tennis—will most likely be provided by Coconut Cove at no extra charge.

THE McGINTYS

The McGintys will no doubt see a reduction in the amount they spend on income tax, which is $12,000 a year. Since Chuck might have to work part-time to help keep himself and Nora afloat, they imagine they might be paying around $6,000 a year in retirement, or $7,200 when you multiply it by their inflation factor of 1.2.

The good news is that their mortgage will be paid off within the next five years, so the $300 a month they're currently paying will be reduced to zero by the time Chuck hopes to throw in the towel at 65.

Since they plan to stay right where they are, there are many expenses they won't have to guess at—these will likely remain exactly the same, except for inflation.

The $200 a month they now pay for heat and utilities will come to $240. It's costing them $360 a year for water, which means that in the future the cost will be $432.

With their kids all settled, the McGintys now spend $75 a month in phone bills, and they expect that cost to remain steady. In future dollars, however, they'll be paying the phone company a total of $90 a month.

The McGintys have never used credit cards, so there are no consumer loans they have to worry about.

As for property taxes, those will at least remain at a shocking $5,000. They hope (but doubt) that the only increase will be through inflation to $6,000.

Currently covered under Chuck's plan at Grumman, the McGintys don't have to pay anything for their health insurance, and (hopefully) that won't change when he turns 65. As for homeowners' insurance, they're not going anywhere, so the $1,000 a year they spend will be the same in retirement, except that when you factor in inflation, the number rises to $1,200. Similarly, Chuck is locked into a whole-life insurance policy for which he pays $200 a year, and that's not changing, either.

In the last chapter I mentioned that one of the reasons Nora wants to remain on Long Island is that she finally has the house decorated the way she'd always dreamed. That means the McGintys won't be spending anything on furnishings. It also means the house requires a relatively stable amount to maintain it, so the $100 a month they now spend on household items will be the same, save for inflation, which could require them to lay out $120 a month instead.

Since it's only the two of them living there, and has been that way for awhile now, the $150 a month they spend on food will be the same in retirement, although inflation could drive the cost up to $180 a month.

Right now, the McGintys shoulder a $1,000 a year deductible on medical bills, and they see no reason for that to change. Of course, they're not thrilled that inflation would force that amount up to $1,200 a year. But they figure they'll cross that bridge when and if they come to it.

As for personal care, both have been going to the same hair salon for twenty years, and they have no intention of switching now. Hence the $50 a month they spend will be close to the same in retirement, with inflation hiking it to only about $60.

The McGintys have simple tastes when it comes to entertainment: they prefer renting movies to paying to see them in the theater, and they treat themselves to breakfast at the diner twice a month. Overall they spend about $50 on entertainment and will continue doing so, except that it could wind up costing them $60 a month with inflation.

As for travel, they spend about $1,000 a year, most of it on gasoline, some of it on trips to see the kids. This won't change when Chuck retires, although inflation could put the figure at $1,200.

As for contributions and gifts, the McGintys give about $200 a year to Catholic Charities, a practice they intend to continue into retirement. With inflation, they'll be giving around $240 a year. They don't spent too much a year on gifts, either—somewhere around $125, all of it on their grandchild. That won't change, either, meaning the yearly cost with inflation will be $150 a year.

A few areas where the McGintys can expect to see a reduction in expenses are clothing, transportation, and education. While Chuck doesn't have to report to work in a suit, he does have to wear a jacket and tie, which is one reason the McGintys spend about $3,000 a year on clothing. They expect that number to drop to $2,000 a year—$2,400 with inflation—as Nora continues to buy clothing and Chuck relies on his existing wardrobe for part-time work and invests in some warm-up suits to lounge around in. Since he will no longer be commuting back and forth to Grumman daily by car, they expect the $160 a month they now pay for gas will be cut in half to $80, or $96 in future dollars.

As is the case with many retirees, Chuck and Nora expect their hobby expenses to rise in retirement. Right now, they spend about $1,000 a year on Chuck's bowling league membership and Nora's knitting yarn, among other things. In retirement, Chuck thinks, he might like to join a gym, so the McGintys estimate that they might be spending $1,500 a year, or $1,800 in inflated dollars.

If you've figured out what you'll need in retirement (with a minimum of math-related trauma, I hope), it's time for the next big step in the process: analyzing where you are now.

WHERE ARE YOU NOW?

Let's hope you've had enough time to recuperate from the trauma of all the math in the previous chapter. You have accomplished an essential task: you've arrived at an estimate of the amount of money you'll need both monthly and annually—in real and inflationary dollars—to live in retirement. If you still haven't recovered, put down this book right now and take a small breather, because your days of wine and calculation are not yet through. In just a few pages, you'll be assessing where you are now, financially speaking. But before you put on the java, pull out the pencil sharpener, and grab the still warm calculator, consider the following.

MAINTAINING YOUR STREAM OF INCOME

In calculating the amount you'll need to live on in retirement, you made an implicit assumption: that you'll be working steadily between now and whenever it is you're retiring. But as everyone knows, guaranteed jobs are as extinct as the dodo. Corporate downsizing is a fact of life. Job security is nonexistent. To survive in today's marketplace, you must be creative, flexible, and capable of constant self-reinvention. Most important, you must direct these abilities toward an ultimate goal: maintaining a steady stream of income. Without a steady income, any dreams of a secure retirement vanish.

There are two components you need to think about when it comes to ensuring your ability to bring home the bacon. One is doing what you can do now to make your current job as secure as possible. The other is learning what it takes to survive as a free agent in the job market, since odds are high you'll be working for a couple of different organizations between now and retirement.

Keeping up appearances

It's true there's no such thing as job security anymore. But that doesn't mean you're completely powerless when it comes to determining whether you'll be staying or receiving a notice of termination. If you're like most people who have been working the same job for a while, you may have fallen into a deadly, enervating routine. You know what your job entails, and you do it—nothing more. The days when you labored enthusiastically to prove your worth are a distant memory. In short, you've become something of a Dilbert.

Unfortunately, this is exactly the opposite of what you should be doing. To help ensure that you're not one of the first given notice should your company downsize, you need to behave as if you're the new kid on the block: ready, willing, and able to roll up your sleeves and prove what an asset you are. Below, a few pointers on reinventing yourself on the job.

First, act as if every day were your first day of work. That means arriving on time with a big smile on your face, ready to face the challenges of the day.

It also means dressing professionally, whether or not your company has a dress-down Friday policy or not. You're trying to convey a message: that you take your job, and your position, very seriously. Slouching around in chinos and a loosened tie won't help your cause.

Having made a conscious effort to dress well, do whatever

it takes to maintain your professional appearance over the course of the workday. If you're a woman, this might mean touching up your makeup and fixing your hair. If you're a man, it could mean keeping an electric shaver in your desk and giving your chin a quick going-over at lunchtime. Regardless of gender, your breath should always be fresh. Forget about loosening your tie, kicking off your heels when your tootsies are under the desk, or slinging your Hugo Boss jacket over the back of your chair. Your goal, pain in the butt though it may be, is to look like a pro at all times.

Not only that, but you need to act like a pro as well. That means being at your desk when the boss walks in, and waving good-bye to the boss in the evening when he or she leaves. It means acting enthusiastic even if yours is the most monotonous or soul-killing job in the organization. Bosses like happy workers. They equate happiness with productivity. Behaving as if you really care about what you're doing can go a long way toward ensuring your position. If the thought of doing this is anathema to you, it's time to find another job.

If you're like most people, you work in a company filled with lots of other folks with whom you interact throughout the course of the day. Titillating as it may be, avoid indulging in company gossip. While it's fine to listen to office dirt (especially since it often contains valuable info that can be pertinent to your job security), don't do any dishing yourself, especially if the company appears headed for hard times. You do not want to be fingered as one of the agitators responsible for spreading panic through the ranks.

Another word about your coworkers: Don't expect them to keep mum on your spruced-up appearance and improved attitude. They will want to know what's up, and may even poke fun at you. Play deaf; they're not the ones you're worried about impressing.

Enhancing job performance

You're looking good and acting happy. But in order to convince your supervisor the change is more than superficial, you need to put your nose to the grindstone and prove you're an asset to the company—one too valuable to let go. How to do this? Read on.

Start by increasing your responsibilities at work, whether voluntarily or when asked. You'll be viewed as a take-charge employee and a hard worker, which is what most companies want.

Work to increase your job skills as well. Many companies offer employees training and education programs; take advantage of them. If your company doesn't, start educating yourself. Brush up on writing, speaking, and computer skills. Increase your knowledge of business by studying an area you're not familiar with. If you're not sure what you should be doing to make yourself more valuable, talk to your boss or the company's human resources person, and ask point blank what she or he thinks you should do. The mere fact that you're seeking to make yourself more valuable will impress either of them no end.

It will also help if you expand your horizons when it comes to knowledge about the company and the industry. Read the company newsletter and the trade papers. Find out what pundits attuned to your industry are saying. This will help you to participate knowledgeably in conversation, and will show you do your homework and care about the future of the business.

Your superiors will also love you to bits if you come up with ways to save them money or time. Time-saving suggestions are especially welcomed by the suits (because it gives them even more time to make even more money).

Last but not least, see if you can't get others to sing your praises to the folks in power. If you have customers or clients, ask them to write letters on your behalf describing what a savvy soul you are. If you don't have a customer base, look to your coworkers, helping them out in any way you can so that when the shoe's on the other foot, they'll help you out, no questions asked.

"Boss, may I speak with you?"

The final element to your transformation on the job is to meet with your superior one on one. Why? Because if he is too thick to have noticed what a great job you're doing or how polished you look, you need to bring it to his attention.

The meeting should be scheduled at your supervisor's convenience. If you can, arrange to meet before work sometime in the middle of the week. If not, rearrange your schedule to make time when your supervisor is available.

Once you've gained admittance to the boss's inner sanctum, don't beat around the bush. Tell him your job is your life and that there's nothing you value more than his opinion of you. Tell him you want to do everything you can to contribute to the company's success, and outline what you've done already. What you're doing, in essence, is trying to get your boss to give you an informal job review while at the same time bringing to his attention your unique value as an employee.

If, God forbid, your boss does point out some areas of job performance where he thinks you're not up to snuff, do not return to your desk and begin composing your suicide note. Instead, try to frame the criticism in positive terms: you've been given an opportunity to improve your performance, and you're going to take it. Once you correct whatever deficiencies you're supposedly guilty of, make another appointment with your boss to make sure he is cognizant of the fact that your work is now superior in all areas. With regular raises and promotions things of the past, you're going to need to sit down with your boss and figure out a way for the two of you to measure your success on the job. If your company doesn't have a performance review system, the best way to do this is to develop a very specific set of goals. In fact, this is now standard policy at many corporations: supervisors are required to lay out specific goals for employees, and employees, in turn, must sign off on the plan, acknowledging that they understand their supervisor's expectations and will work toward those goals. Whether your company has an established policy or not, once your goals are achieved, you can use them as evidence of your success, which will help you either negotiate a pay increase or move on to another project.

OUT IN THE MARKETPLACE

Hard as it may be to contemplate, today's corporate climate virtually guarantees that, at one point or another, you're going to find yourself looking for a new job. Is this a drag? Yes. Life would be much less stressful if we all had job security the way folks used to. But we don't—which is why you should periodically reassess your work role and shift your focus from your employer to yourself.

In today's job market, it's each employee for him- or herself. No longer are people hired with an eye toward keeping them on indefinitely; rather, individuals are being hired on the basis of job skills they're able to bring to specific projects. If you've got the skills, you get the job. When the project's done, you either find another project to work on within the company, or find a different company to work for. Your value is determined by your performance on your most recent project.

I know it sounds frightening, but it's really not. It actually is an opportunity to be master of your own employment fate. But in order to do that, you need to be familiar with how to play what seems to be an everchanging game. Here's how.

Redefine who you are

Most people define themselves not only by what they do, but by where they work. For example, if someone were to ask the Pope about himself, he might say, "I'm head of the Catholic Church and I work at the Vatican."

Such a rigid definition is a mistake. As a freelancer (which is how you need to think of yourself from now on), you should focus on yourself and your skills, not on whose employ you're in while using those skills. Thus, when asked the same question as above, the Pope should respond, "I'm a priest currently guiding all the world's Catholics."

Assess your skills

What does your individual bundle of skills consist of? If you haven't taken the time to sit down and figure out all the tasks you're capable of doing and all the successes you've achieved, do it now.

Start by coming up with a list of all your personal and professional achievements. Personal achievements are important, because they often incorporate skills you haven't had a chance to utilize at work. Compose a couple of sentences about each achievement as if you were explaining what you did to your spouse. For example, let's say Mitch Kahn wants to draft a list of his achievements. For a personal achievement he might say to Sheryl, "I organized the Ann Arbor Pee Wee Soccer League and coached our daughter's soccer team." For a professional achievement he might say, "I supervised training of the new sales staff, created the training program, and implemented it."

Leave no stone unturned in this exercise. Make it as comprehensive as you can. When you're done, go through each statement and write down every verb you used to describe your actions. Mitch, for example, would write down "organized," "coached," "supervised," "created," and "implemented."

The words you write down are, in fact, your skills, just as the achievements you've talked about are concrete documentation of them. This exercise is more than just a self-assessment tool: it can also be used to create a new résumé.

Get mercenary

Forget about spiritual fulfillment, or expressing your values, or any of that New Age claptrap. Harsh as it may sound, you should look to your job to provide you with one thing and one thing only: a steady source of income. In other words, you're in the game to make money.

Does this mean you should change your name to Ebenezer Scrooge? Not at all. But it does mean that you should focus on finding ways to let other areas of your life—your family, your hobbies, your volunteer work—fulfill you spiritually, and allow your job to serve the purpose for which it's been designed: increasing your monthly bank balance. By the way, cultivating those outside interests now will set you up for quite an active and fulfilling retirement.

Develop bifocal vision

Focusing on the task at hand when it comes to work is important. But as a freelancer, you need to extend your vision beyond the present; you need to be concerned with how what you're doing now will impact your chances of landing another job. You also need to be concerned not only with your own company, but with the industry at large. And beyond that, you need to be aware of what's going on in the economy, not only nationally but internationally.

In other words, never stop your search for the next job. This doesn't mean slacking off in the job you currently hold. It simply means engaging in some long-term, strategic career planning. To this end, get in the habit of collecting the business cards of whomever you meet, whether they're involved in your industry or not. Keep a finger on the pulse of what's happening in your community by getting involved. If your current job evaporates, any one of those people you've encountered might be instrumental in helping you find your next job.

INCOME: WILL IT RISE OR FALL?

While the competition in the job market is fierce, this doesn't mean you should take any old offer that comes your way. As companies try to keep costs down, more and more of them are being forced to pay competitive wages to attract highly skilled workers. With unemployment expected to continue its decline, wages are projected to rise roughly 6 percent a year for the next four years or so, according to the WEFA (Wharton Econometric Forecasting Association) Group, a leading economic information and forecast firm.

While that's good news, the bad news is that any pay increase you experience probably won't be coming in the form of an annual raise. Instead, your company might offer you one of the compensation strategies cited below.

Profit sharing

Long a fixture on the corporate scene, this is where employees get a piece of the company's profits, often in the form of a year-end cash bonus.

A more focused version of this is "gain sharing," where employees are entitled to only that share of profits that are the result of increased productivity. If productivity remains static, then it's tough luck on the worker ants. But if productivity raises as profits soar, everyone gets to partake of the financial fruit of their own increased labor.

In addition, some companies have started basing bonuses on individual or group performance rather than the company's overall productivity—so thinking and acting as an entrepreneur can have a direct effect on your annual income.

Skill-based pay

This is just what it sounds like: the more skills you possess, the bigger your paycheck.

The goal is to create a flexible workforce capable of wearing many different hats, all of which will hopefully benefit the employer and allow him an edge over the competition.

One-time bonus

Usually paid in cash, these lump-sum payments have all but replaced the traditional raise in some companies.

Workers as part-owners

It's not hard to see why companies would love this one. If you owned stock in the company you work for, wouldn't you bust your butt to make sure the company's bottom line was fabulous? Employee ownership has been around since 1974, and recent studies have found that in some instances, productivity has gone through the roof after an employee stock ownership program, or ESOP, was implemented. Unfortunately, many ESOPs are established in exchange for pay concessions from workers (i.e., lower take-home pay as you buy stock with money deducted from your paycheck).

Two-tiered pay

This is a scheme where workers hired after a certain date get paid less than senior workers.

It's a great plan if you're a fat cat with a big corner office who's been on the job for ten years, but for new employees, it does little but breed discontent, as time goes on and some individuals continue to be paid less for doing the same work as their counterparts.

Not surprisingly, these pay schemes reinforce an important fact mentioned earlier: that there's no such thing as job security. Not only are steadily rising wages (in the form of regular raises) unlikely, but these schemes are designed to ensure that the other elements of your compensation package remain unaffected. Good thing you're a freelancer, willing to be flexible and indulge in some bifocal vision. Otherwise, you'd be in real trouble.

BREAKING DOWN CURRENT SAVINGS AND INVESTMENTS

You now know what you need to do in order to remain employed so you can fund that retirement. But in order to get to where you want to go—namely, a comfortable retirement—you need to know exactly where you are now. Only then will you be able to map out the best route to help you achieve your dreams. The first step? Calculating your current savings, investments, and other assets.

Assets are everything you own. A complete listing should include:

- cash on hand
- savings account balance
- checking account balance
- certificates of deposit (CDs)
- mutual fund accounts
- portfolio of stocks and bonds
- IRAs/401(k)s/SEPs
- savings bonds
- life insurance (cash value)
- accounts receivable (money you're owed)
- house (market value)
- other real estate
- car (resale value)

You should also include the market value of personal property, such as:

- furnishings
- jewelry
- electronic equipment (computers, camcorders, etc.)
- clothing
- art and collectibles

Just as you did in the previous chapter, get out a pencil, paper, and calculator and tabulate what your total assets, including savings and investments, are in annual terms. A few tips to keep in mind:

It's up to you how simple or detailed your list is. What's important is that it gives you enough information to determine where you are now, and a starting point from which to measure future financial progress.

Painful as it may be, it's in your best interest to be honest with yourself. Assets are worth what you can sell them for—not what you originally paid for them.

Do not forget to convert your insurance policies to their cash equivalent for this exercise. A call to your insurance company will enable you to get the figures. Similarly, your employer should be able to provide you with the value of your pension rights or your share in a profit-sharing plan.

Household furnishings are worth only what they'd bring on the secondhand market—unless, of course, they're antiques. If you own any original works of art, be sure to include their value in your calculations.

Any real estate you own, including the house you're living in, is worth the current market value minus what it would cost you to sell it. To find out what your house is currently worth, talk to a real estate agent or get listings of homes of comparable value in your area.

Finally, stocks and bonds should be valued at current market price.

To help give you an idea of what an asset total might look like, let's turn to our three couples.

THE HARPERS

At present, the Harpers carry around $100 each in their wallets, so their cash-on-hand number is $200. Their savings account balance reads $1,000, and their checking account balance $4,000. When it comes to investments, they've got one ninety-day certificate of deposit worth $2,500, plus $2,000 in a growth-and-income mutual fund. Sarah participates in a 401(k) through work; currently estimated to be worth $5,000, that money is also invested in a growth-and-income mutual fund.

The cash value on their life insurance policy is $750. There's no money owed them, and they own no other real estate apart from their condo, which is worth $300,000 in the current market. The resale value on their car, according to their mechanic, is $12,000.

When it comes to personal property, the furniture in their home is worth about $10,000. The jewelry Sarah has inherited from her grandmother, including a rare and beautiful cameo, is worth $5,000. Tim's home computer, printer, and fax machine are worth $5,000, which is half the value of the clothing of both Harpers, which comes to $10,000. Fond of antiques, Sarah and Tim have managed to acquire a few pieces worth about $2,000 altogether.

Their total in investments, savings, and other assets? $359,450.

THE KAHNS

Between them, Mitch and Sheryl have $500 in petty cash, most of it in Mitch's hands since he spends a good deal of time wining and dining potential Toshinko clients. As far as their savings account goes, they've got a balance of $2,500, and their checking account balance, like the Harpers', is $4,000. Their only "investment" is Sheryl's 401(k) plan at work, where she has $8,000 invested in a growth-and-income mutual fund.

Years ago, Mother Kahn gave them a savings bond when they first got married, and that's now worth $250. No one owes them any money, and their life insurance policies have no cash values. The current market value of their house is $125,000. Mitch has a company car, while the minivan Sheryl drives around is worth about $2,000.

As far as personal property goes, the Kahns have $15,000 worth of furnishings and about $8,000 in jewelry, thanks to Sheryl's refusal to accept anything less than a two-carat diamond engagement ring. Mitch's laptop is worth $2,000, and the clothes on their backs and in their closets come to

$15,000. Between Mitch's antique Ping golf clubs and the Miró lithograph their best friends, the Levines, gave them for their tenth anniversary, the value of their art and collectibles is $5,000.

Add up the numbers and you'll see the Kahns' total of savings, investments, and other assets is $187,250.

THE McGINTYS

The McGintys have very little cash on hand: $100 ($60 in Chuck's wallet and $40 in Nora's purse). Chuck participates in a Christmas club through Grumman; right now they have $300 in a savings account. Luckily, they do have a bit more than that in checking: $2,000. They have no CDs, no mutual funds, and no stock and bond portfolios. Worse, they don't even have an IRA, a 401(k), or an SEP. (We'll take a look at these retirement plans and others in the next chapter.) What the McGintys do have is a $300 savings bond, a long-ago anniversary gift from Nora's sister Eileen.

No one owes them any money. Their house is worth $225,000, and the resale value of their car, a late-model Ford Taurus, is $10,000. Since they've never cared for lavish furnishings, the furniture in their home is worth only $6,000. They have no equipment to speak of, but Nora does have some nice jewelry, valued at about $3,000. Since Chuck is the only one who has to worry about dressing up, their clothing is valued at $7,000. They've never been very big on art and collectibles, either, although Nora's Hummel collection could probably fetch $250.

Hence the McGintys' total assets, including savings and investments, come to $253,950.

BREAKING DOWN YOUR LIABILITIES

Simply put, your liabilities are the amounts of money you owe. A complete listing of liabilities should include:

- balance due on your mortgage
- balance due on your credit cards
- balance due on student loans
- balance due on home equity loans
- balance due on your car loan
- amount owed on your life insurance premium

Just as you did with your assets, tally your liabilities and come up with a number. Here's how our three couples fared.

THE HARPERS

The Harpers currently owe $200,000 on their mortgage, and their credit card debt is $1,000. They're free and clear when it comes to student and home equity loans, but they do owe a bit on that Volvo of theirs, to the tune of $6,000. As far as insurance premiums go, they owe $600. So what's the damage? $207,600.

THE KAHNS

The balance due on the Kahns' mortgage is $55,000. They owe $500 on their credit cards, which isn't too bad, especially when it's compared to what they owe on education loans for their daughter: $60,000. But that's it for their liabilities. The grand total they owe the world? $115,500.

THE McGINTYS

Last but not least come the McGintys. Lucky them: they owe only $5,000 on their mortgage. They've never used credit cards. Their only other debt is the $200 they owe on Chuck's life insurance premium. The total figure for Chuck and Nora's liabilities? $5,200.

CALCULATING YOUR NET WORTH

Now that you know how much you've got in investments, savings, and other assets, and are also painfully aware of how much money you owe, it's time to figure out your net worth. It's easy to do: simply subtract your liabilities from your assets. The number you're left with is your net worth, or what you're truly worth in dollars at this minute in time.

Let's calculate the net worth of our three couples. For the Harpers, we need to subtract $207,600 from $359,450 to see that Tim and Sarah's net worth is $151,850. The Kahns' net worth is $71,750 ($187,250 minus $115,500), and the McGintys' net worth is $248,750 ($253,950 minus $5,200).

GETTING THERE FROM HERE

You know where you want to get to in retirement, and now that you've figured out your net worth, you know exactly where you're starting from. But don't forget that you'll probably be getting some financial help along the way, in the form of Social Security and whatever income you'll be receiving from your own savings or your job when you retire. Both need to be figured into your calculations, since they'll be used to help you cover your expenses in retirement.

For example: Tim Harper doesn't expect any pension from his law firm when he retires, but between them, the Harpers are counting on $10,000 a year from Social Security.

Mitch Kahn, on the other hand, will receive a pension from Toshinko to the tune of $30,000 a year, and together, he and Sheryl will get $12,000 a year from Social Security. (By contacting your local Social Security office, you can get an estimate of what you'll collect from Social Security.) Do the math and you can see that there's going to be $42,000 a year coming in to help them cover expenses.

As for the McGintys, Chuck is counting on $35,000 a year from Grumman upon retirement. Like the Kahns, he and Nora will get $12,000 a year in Social Security checks. So when all is said and done, the McGintys are looking at $47,000 a year to help defray the cost of living in retirement.

Before you get too excited about this "found" money that will help you achieve the retirement of your dreams, allow me to break some bad news: Unless you're Donald Trump, there's still going to be a gap (probably a huge one) between your current resources and your eventual needs in retirement. That gap is what you need to fill between now and retirement day to make sure you can, indeed, retire the way you've planned.

To figure out how big that gap is going to be, use this simple method:

1. Referring back to last chapter, take your estimated annual income in retirement (in inflated dollars).
2. Take your estimated Social Security income and your estimated pension income and add them together.
3. Subtract this combined income figure from the number you wrote down for expenses in step 1.
4. Take that remainder and multiply it by the personal inflation factor you used in Chapter 5, based on the inflation factor table on page 61.
5. The result is the amount of income you'll need in retirement that you don't have covered.

Based on historical analysis of how every type of investment has performed from the stock market crash of 1929 to the bull market of 1997, conservative, pragmatic financial planners believe that for every $1,000 of annual income you'll need to fund retirement, you should have at least $17,000 in savings and investments in order to keep up with inflation. Obviously you would need less if your money was invested aggressively and those investments worked out. On the other hand, you would need even more if you invested conservatively and your money was slow to grow. The $17K figure is an average, based on the typical blended, diversified investment portfolio. If you're planning on retiring at age 65, multiply the figure from step 5 by 17 to see how much investment savings you're going to need in inflated dollars. Those planning for early retirement should multiply by 20 to make up for those years of lost compound interest.

Let's see how much money our three couples are going to need to save between now and retirement, using the above formula.

As we saw in Chapter 5, Tim and Sarah Harper projected that their annual retirement income need, in inflated dollars, will be around $196,875. Subtract the $10,000 they're anticipating from Social Security, and the figure goes down to $186,875. Multiply that number by the Harpers' inflation factor of 2.1, and we see the number skyrocket to $392,437.50. But wait; we're not done. Since Tim is planning early retirement, he needs to multiply by 20 rather than 17 to figure out how much the Harpers will need in savings and investments to keep up with inflation. That number—and believe me, it's as shocking to the Harpers as it is to you—is $7,848,750.

The Kahns need less, but not by much. Their projected annual income need in retirement is $172,500. If you subtract from that the $42,000 they expect to get from Social Security and Mitch's pension combined, the number dips down to $130,500. But when you multiply it by their inflation factor of 2.3, it jumps up to $300,150. As if that's not bad enough, multiply it by the standard 17, and we see the Kahns will need savings and investments of at least $5,102,550 by the time they retire.

Now, to the McGintys. Chuck and Nora figured they would need $54,000 yearly to be able to live in retirement. Combine their expected Social Security payments and Chuck's pension from Grumman and you come up with $47,000. When they subtract that from their projected need they come up with a gap of $7,000. Not too bad. But when you multiply it by 1.2, it rises to $8,400, and when you multiply that by 17, the final number reads $142,800. That's a lot of fishnagles for them to come up with in five years, when Chuck plans on retiring.

If you're like most people, you probably came close to coronary arrest after running your numbers through the above formula and figuring out the gap that needs to be covered in your finances. In fact, you probably think it's impossible to raise that kind of money. Well, it's not. With the right investment tools and a little self-discipline you can get from where you are to where you want to be. The first step in the process? Attitude, baby, attitude—which, not coincidentally, happens to be the subject of the next chapter.

7

ATTITUDE

I'll say it again, covering that phenomenally huge financial gap between what you have now and what you'll need in retirement is not an insurmountable task—provided you have the right tools, and the right attitude.

FIRST THINGS FIRST

Most of us pursue our financial goals in a fairly predictable sequence. The first major investment we make is in a home, and that is followed by saving for our children's education. Next we set about saving for retirement, while at the same time trying to build up our assets so that when we die, our heirs will be left with something.

People tend to pursue the early goals—buying a home and saving for college—sequentially, since, being young, they find it nearly impossible to pursue them simultaneously; there are just too many other demands on their not-yet-maximized stream of income. However, many people, when they are older and more established, try to accomplish the latter two goals—funding retirement and building an estate for heirs—simultaneously. News flash, folks: It's going to be mighty tough for you to both fund a decent retirement and leave behind an estate.

Not that it can't be done—the Harpers, for example, who happen to be young and pulling down decent salaries, intend to try it. But for most of us, leaving an estate is something we should concern ourselves with only after we've got our retirement program in place. It doesn't make any sense to set aside funds for your adult kids before you've set them aside for yourself. If you don't take care of your own needs you may need to turn to your kids for financial help. So helping yourself is, in fact, helping them.

I'm suggesting that in order to bridge that tremendous gap you've discovered, you need to temporarily set aside your vision of providing your children with a generous inheritance and concentrate all your energies on having enough money for retirement. I'm not saying you should give up your estate-building dreams . . . just put them on hold for a while. Once you've taken care of your own needs you'll be free to turn back to any estate-building goals you may have.

ACCEPT MEASURED RISKS

If you're serious about wanting to make your money work for you to the extent that you'll be able to close that financial gap, then you'll need to be willing to assume some risk. It's simply an immutable law of personal finance: The greater the potential reward, the greater the potential risk. In other words, the farther you're willing to stick your financial neck out, the faster your money will grow.

However, that doesn't mean you should jump into commodities and options—two incredibly risky investments I'll explain later in the book—because you've got a giant gap between your dreams and your reality. In order to maximize your chances to succeed, and to sleep at night, you need to take *measured* risk. That means you look, and look again, before leaping.

There are two key components that must be taken into account when contemplating financial risk:

- how much money you need to save between now and when you plan to retire
- how much time you have to save it

Generally speaking, the younger you are, the more financial risk you can assume. Why? Because you've got more years ahead of you in which to recoup any losses you might experience.

Thus, investing primarily in the stock market makes sense when you're young. (We'll talk more about this in the next two chapters). Though stocks can behave erratically in the short term, over the long haul they have grown more money faster than any other investment tool around. This is why the Harpers have some of their money in stock mutual funds.

If you're older, however, investing primarily in stocks isn't necessarily the wisest choice. If the market should drop just as you're about to retire, your odds of recuperating from such financial losses are pretty slim. You simply wouldn't have the time.

Therefore, the risks you take with your money if you're older should be less than those you take when you're younger. That's why so many older individuals invest primarily in bonds: they tend to be very stable in the short term (but unlikely to grow much in the long term).

If you've been doing the financial exercises provided in this book, then you're well aware of how much money you need to accrue between now and retirement as well as whether time is on your side. That means you're ready for the next step in the process, which is figuring out the best investment strategy for your money—or how much risk you should assume.

Unfortunately, there are many people who get the heebie-jeebies at the mere thought of risking any of their money. If you're one of those people, you've got two choices: you either get a grip and learn more about financial risk-taking so the thought doesn't scare you, or else you go back to the two factors mentioned above—how much money you need to save and how long you have to save it—and you change one of them.

For example, Chuck and Nora McGinty need to figure out a way to come up with $142,800 over the next five years. Being older, they're not about to invest in anything very risky, so the chances of their being able to bridge that gap—unless they win the New York State Lottery—aren't great. What they need to do is go back to their blueprint for retirement and ask: What can we change so that number isn't insurmountable?

For the McGintys there are two possible solutions: they can leave Long Island and move to a part of the country where the cost of living is lower, or Chuck (and maybe Nora) can keep working past age 65, increasing their income in "retirement." Either solution would result in a smaller financial gap to be bridged.

The mistake that many people make is holding fast to a rigid set of goals for retirement while remaining steadfastly unwilling to assume the level of financial risk required to reach those goals. Success can be obtained only if you're willing to do what it takes to achieve your dreams. If you're not willing to do what's required—or if for some reason you determine that you can't—then you need to go back and rethink your goals.

*   *   *

The key to growing your money is finding the match between your goals and the amount of risk you're willing to take. But to do that, you need to examine the different strategies and techniques available to help you invest for retirement. Read on.

8

PENSIONS AND OTHER RETIREMENT PLANS

Unless you've been living in a cave, you've no doubt heard about the many different retirement plans out there: Keoghs, IRAs, 401(k)s, ESOPs—the list is long and growing. But for many people, these plans are little more than names. Those individuals have no idea how the plans work, how they differ, which ones their company might offer, and which require the individual to take a more proactive role. That's the job of this chapter: to help you sort through the different retirement plans so you can make informed decisions about funding your retirement.

Pensions are nothing new. In fact, the first American pension plans can be traced back more than 350 years, to the settlers of the first colony at Plymouth, who established a military pension in 1636. The first corporate pension plan was created in 1875 by American Express. Today, it's estimated that two-thirds of the workforce is covered by some form of company-sponsored pension.

That number seems high, until you realize that not everyone takes advantage of the pension plans employers offer. In fact, it's believed that a whopping 60 percent of the current workforce aren't saving for retirement through company-sponsored plans. While some employees in that 60 percent don't have a company-sponsored plan available to them, many do, and still fail to take part. One reason is that many employees simply don't understand the plans, so they don't bother to participate. That's a shame, because company-sponsored retirement plans can make the difference between not having enough money to fund retirement, and being able to pursue your retirement dreams.

While pensions—whether funded by you, your employer, or both—may not pay out enough to completely cover the cost of your retirement, they are the best first step. That's because they generally offer you the best chance to maximize your money, either by being tax-deferred or by being matched by your employer. Everyone, regardless of age, income level, or work-life plans, should begin his or her retirement planning by taking maximum advantage of all available pension options.

EMPLOYER-SPONSORED PENSIONS

Before storming into the personnel office and demanding information about your company's 401(k) plan, a few facts.

First, your salary has nothing to do with whether or not you can participate in your company's retirement plan (if it has one). Whether you're earning megabucks or just making ends meet, company pension plans are available to all employees—that's the law.

But what if your company doesn't offer a retirement pension plan? No problem: you can create one for yourself. Conventional methods include opening an individual retirement account, or IRA, or investing in a tax-deferred annuity. Don't start palpitating if you don't know what I'm talking about; all will be revealed.

Even if your company does offer a pension plan, that doesn't mean you can't look out for your own interests by opening your own IRA as well. While there are rules about how much money you can contribute annually and still deduct from your taxes, keep in mind that any money invested in an IRA will grow, tax-free, until it's time to withdraw it.

Qualified versus nonqualified

In the course of your work life, you might have heard of qualified and nonqualified plans, but didn't know the difference. A *qualified plan* is one where the employer both sets up and contributes to the employees' pension plans. Why, that's awfully generous of the company, you might be thinking. Not really. These plans allow employers to receive some mighty hefty tax breaks. So much for corporate altruism.

Nonqualified plans are those employers set up but usually don't contribute to, since they don't qualify for tax deductions. This doesn't affect how your money grows, however. Whether your company offers a qualified or nonqualified plan, the money invested in your plan will grow, tax-deferred, regardless.

Defined-benefit versus defined-contribution

Defined-benefit plans are those in which the company for which you work does all the funding of your retirement plan. You don't have to put in a penny. But these plans also have a hitch: you don't have any say in how the money in your plan is invested. It's entirely up to the big guys. How much money you actually receive at retirement is based on a formula that takes into account your salary compensation, as well as how long you've worked for the company. When retirement day rolls around, your monthly retirement income is calculated and then paid out according to your company's formula.

Most companies use one of three formulas for calculating employee retirement benefits: final pay, career average, or flat benefit. Though the formulas are different, each takes into account the two factors mentioned above—your compensation and how long you've been a wage slave.

You're not eligible to participate in a defined-benefit plan unless you've worked at the company a certain number of years—in other words, until you're vested. The rules for vesting differ from employer to employer, but all are based on the length of time you've worked for your employer.

The most commonly used vesting timetables are gradual vesting and cliff vesting. With *gradual vesting,* your qualification for benefits occurs in stages. For example, if you've been with the company two years, you might be 20 percent vested in it; after four years, the number might rise to 40 percent. This usually goes on for seven years, after which point you're considered fully vested. With *cliff vesting,* you're considered fully vested once you pass the five-year mark.

One possible drawback to defined-benefit plans is that, because they depend on the employer's wisdom and goodwill, they aren't guaranteed. There have been all too many instances of companies tapping into the money set aside for their employees' retirements or investing it poorly, and having to renege on their pension promises. Remember, a promise, even from an apparently solid company, is only as good as the honesty and integrity of its owner or board of directors. And unfortunately, sometimes that's not good enough.

In the case of *defined-contribution plans,* the employer, employee, or both make contributions to a retirement account. You're probably already familiar with the names of some of these plans: 401(k)s, 403(b)s, ESOPs, and SEPs (simplified employee pensions).

Defined-contribution plans are very popular with companies today. It's not hard to understand why, at least from the employer's perspective. For one thing, the company doesn't have to shoulder the entire burden of funding your retirement plan. For another, the company isn't solely responsible for deciding how the moneys in your fund are invested; you have a say in the matter. This frees the company from any potential liability as well as from total responsibility.

In fact, in the case of what's known as employee-directed defined-contribution plans, you're responsible for all investment decisions regarding your pension. This is great if you know something about making long-term investment choices. But if you don't, you could wind up with a lot less money at retirement than you anticipated.

A PENSION INVESTIGATION CHECKLIST

Below are some questions you should ask your employer, or your company's employee benefits representative, about your plan:

- What's the name of the plan being offered?
- Will I have to pay any fees to participate in this plan?
- As simply as you can, would you please define the plan as well as what it means for me as an employee?
- Do I have any choice as to where and how I can invest my money in this plan? Can I change my mind about those choices anywhere along the line? And if I do, are there any costs and fees that will be passed on to me for doing so?
- What are those choices? Do you have printed material on the different choices that I can take with me?
- What is the maximum I can invest in the program annually? Can that money be deducted automatically from my paycheck?
- Will the company be making any matching contribution to the plan? If so, how much?
- How well have the investments available to me in this plan performed in the past? What sources can I use to compare how these investments have performed so I know which investments are worthwhile?
- If I leave the company, does my defined contribution money go with me? Can I leave it here? What are the advantages and disadvantages of each choice?
- Must I contribute annually? Or can I occasionally stop making contributions depending upon my financial situation?

• If I have any more questions about the plan, who is the most appropriate person to speak to?

THE ADVANTAGES OF DEFINED-CONTRIBUTION PLANS

Today, most employers are opting for defined-contribution plans rather than defined-benefit plans. While this puts more of a burden on you, it does come with some advantages.

As is the case with any investment, how well a defined-contribution plan performs is contingent on how much and how long your employer and/or you have contributed to the plan, how expertly the pension moneys were invested, and how well the stock market performed during the investment period.

Even with these variables, defined-contribution plans have a lot going for them. For one thing, if your money is managed properly, it's possible for you to rake in big bucks come retirement time. For another, the longer you participate in such a plan, the broader may be the scope of choices available to you as to how and where the money is invested.

Another advantage is that, since you're at least partly responsible for the investment strategy behind your plan, there's less of a chance that it will be used more to the company's advantage than to your own. You may not have the financial expertise of your company's comptroller, let's say, but you do have your best interests at heart.

Equally appealing when it comes to defined-contribution plans is that all employee contributions are vested immediately. This means that if you take a job with another employer, the money you've put into the plan moves with you. In general, money in your defined-contribution plan is handled in one of three ways when you get a new job: it's either placed in a new retirement plan via a rollover (this simply means taking money from one retirement account and putting it in another; you don't incur any taxes or penalties), or disbursed to you in a lump-sum distribution, or it stays with your old employer until you're ready to retire.

Playing it too safe

Before I go any further, I think it's important to say a few words about one of the major problems faced by people who actually take advantage of the defined-contribution plan offered by their employer. Many financial planners feel that because of people's aversion to risk, employees' investments don't always make the money they could.

Going for what's safe might feel the most comfortable, but it's probably not going to give you the biggest return. For example, over 50 percent of people invest the money in their 401(k)s in insurance products investing in fixed-income securities, where the long-term return is subject to both interest rates and inflation. What they should be doing instead is putting more of their money into stocks, which have a proven history of providing better returns than any other investment. Yet only 25 percent of people participating in defined-contribution plans own any stock or stock funds, and only 3.7 percent have half or more of their defined contribution investments in stock or stock funds.

Okay, with all that information under our belts, let's take a closer look at the most commonly used defined-contribution plans.

401(k)s

401(k)s are defined-contribution plans in which money is taken directly from your salary and placed in a tax-deferred retirement plan. In most cases, the decision as to how the money in the plan is to be invested is yours. (Stop sweating. By the time you're done with the next few chapters, you'll be a financial whiz.)

The most attractive thing about 401(k)s—besides the obvious fact that they force you to save for retirement—is that you don't have to pay taxes on the money you've contributed to the plan until retirement. Thus, the more money you put into a 401(k), the lower your taxable salary, the less tax you pay, and the faster your money grows. Sounds great—except that the folks at Social Security still expect you to pay tax on the full amount of your wages, including the money you've sheltered in the 401(k).

Another attractive component to 401(k)s is the "free money" they often provide in the form of matching employer contributions. These can sometimes go as high as 50 cents for every dollar you yourself contribute. That's found money, mate, and those contributions can go a long way in helping you feather your retirement nest.

Unfortunately, that "found money" is only yours if you stay with the company. Should you decide to take another job, 100 percent of the money you put into the account is yours, but the money your employer has put into it may or may not go with you, depending upon company policy. If you're looking for another job, ask about your company's policy.

As to where your 401(k) money can be invested, there are probably a number of different options offered, including various mutual funds, depending on the terms of the plan.

While I strongly encourage you to participate in your company's plan, the truth is 401(k)s are not without flaws. There are limits to the amount you can contribute annually. In 1997, an employee was allowed to contribute up to 15 percent of his or her salary or $9,500, whichever is less. In addition, there's no universal 401(k) plan. The plans vary from company to company, which means you might work for a firm that contributes to the plan, while your sister might work for a firm that doesn't.

Lastly, you can't touch the money in your 401(k) without paying penalties, until you're 59½. Dip into it sooner and the taxman's going to be banging on your door, demanding you pay a 10 percent penalty. You're also penalized if you leave the money in too long, or if you take out too much during any given year.

By the way, the name 401(k) comes from the number of the paragraph in the IRS code that refers to the plans.

403(b)s

403(b)s are just like 401(k)s, except they're for people who work for charitable or nonprofit organizations, such as social service agencies and churches.

Section 403(b) plans work like 401(k)s in that your share of the money to be contributed is deducted directly from your salary. In some cases, your employer will contribute to the plan as well. Whether he does or not, most employees using 403(b)s are usually forbidden from contributing more than 5 percent of their annual salary to the plan.

As with 401(k)s, you make the investment selections for 403(b)s after receiving information on investment options from your employer. Usually there is a wide range of choices available, and in most instances, taxes are deferred on both your contribution and your employer's until you decide to withdraw the money.

Unfortunately, 403(b)s are also similar to 401(k)s in their drawbacks. You are required to pay Social Security taxes on your full salary, and how well your 403(b) performs is contingent on the investments you've chosen.

ESOPs

Employee stock option plans, or ESOPs, are planned investments in the stock of your company. The employer's thoughts run something like this: You and your fellow employees are more likely to bust your tails working for the company if higher productivity means you, too, will share in the company's financial success. It's been estimated that over 11.4 million employees in this country are participating in ESOP plans.

One obvious drawback to ESOPs is that since the company is offering itself, in essence, as the investment, you have very little control. If the company is doing great and stock prices are high when you decide to retire, you could luck out financially. But what if the company's not doing so hot? Then neither will you when payout time comes.

This is why it's important to diversify when it comes to investments, especially if you're part of an ESOP plan and your only investment for retirement is in company stock. Putting all your financial eggs in one basket can be a disaster. So while you should take advantage of an ESOP if your company offers one, be sure you look into other investment options on your own as well.

SELF-FUNDED PLANS

If your company doesn't offer either a defined-benefit or a defined-contribution pension plan, don't give up. You can open up a retirement account on your own. Similarly, if you're self-employed, you can set up your own pension plan. And, even if you've got a pension from work, you can add more to your retirement bundle by opening up additional self-funded accounts. Here are the major types of self-funded plans:

Keoghs

If you're self-employed, then a tax-deferred Keogh might be the way to go. Not only are Keoghs available to those who are entirely self-employed, but they're also there for folks who moonlight, which means it's possible for you to be investing in your company's 401(k) plan while simultaneously socking away the money you make on the side selling knitted baby booties at craft fairs. Like other pension plans explained above, Keoghs can be either defined-benefit or defined-contribution plans, or both. At present, there are four different types of Keogh plans available.

First, there are *profit-sharing Keoghs,* in which you can contribute and deduct up to 13.04 percent of your self-employment adjusted gross income up to $30,000. One of the nice things about this type of Keogh is that you decide how much or how little money you want to put in each year. If you have a bad year, you don't have to put in any at all.

Next, there are *money-purchase Keoghs,* where the maximum that can be contributed is up to 25 percent of your annual self-employed adjusted gross income, with a ceiling of $30,000. The bad part? Once you pick a percentage, you have to stick with it. If God forbid no one wants to buy baby booties one year and you're unable to meet the specified payment, the IRS posse will come looking for you. (In some rare cases the IRS will let you change the level of your contribution if business is bad, but you can't count on it.)

Another type of Keogh is what's known as a *combination Keogh*. This is a money-purchase and profit-sharing Keogh combined, giving you the best of both worlds. You can make the largest possible contribution, while at the same time having the flexibility to pay in the minimum—or nothing—if business isn't going well.

Here's how the combo Keogh works. First, you set up a money-purchase plan with a guaranteed annual payment of whatever percent you choose. Then, you establish a separate profit-sharing plan to receive whatever money you bring in above that established percentage. It's not uncommon for people to start off with a profit-sharing Keogh and add the money-purchase plan later in the game, when (hopefully) they're making more money.

Last but not least, there's what's known as a *defined-benefit Keogh,* designed to provide you with a fixed annual income when you retire. With defined-benefit Keoghs, the ball is completely in your court: you pick the annual pension you want, then contribute whatever amount is needed to achieve your goal. In some instances, you're allowed to contribute up to 100 percent of your self-employment salary annually.

The only hitch is that figuring out what to pay in each year is easier said than done. In fact, it's been known to induce migraine, which might be why the law requires you to see an actuary annually to review your plan and determine how much you have to put away in the upcoming year to meet your projected payout at the end of your employment road. A copy of the actuary's report must accompany your tax return. Seeing the actuary ain't free, nor is it cheap, and the same is true of establishing and maintaining this type of Keogh. However, should your income drop, you can dissolve the Keogh immediately and roll the money over into an IRA.

Most people maintain a single Keogh account, although it is possible to contribute to different Keoghs established to do different things, as long as you don't exceed the annual ceiling. While you can use a Keogh to invest in just about anything, for maximum financial flexibility it's advisable to open a Keogh with a mutual fund group. It's also wise to have a fixed amount of money withdrawn from your bank account each month that goes directly into the Keogh. This will force you to save money you might otherwise be tempted to spend elsewhere.

No matter what kind of Keogh you have, you'll be penalized if you try to take money out of it before you're 59½, and withdrawals are mandatory when you turn 70. But Keoghs differ from other plans in that you can continue putting money into a Keogh after age 70½, and you can also borrow against funds accumulated in the plan if you need to. (There are a zillion restrictions, of course.)

At this point a question inevitably arises: What if I run a small business, meaning I'm self-employed, but I also have employees? The answer is that your employees can be included in your Keogh plan as well. If you contribute 20 percent of your earnings to the plan, then you've got to put 20 percent of each of your employees' earnings into the plan. Remember that actuary mentioned above? Well, he or she will also be the one determining how much you'll be contributing to your employees' Keoghs, based on your business's net profit.

SEPs

Another option for the self-employed, or for the owner of a small company with employees, is a SEP, short for simplified employee pension. SEPs function much like Keoghs and are adored by small business owners, since they leave it up to the employees to manage their own accounts. This saves employers money, since they don't have to pay someone to administer the program. They only have contribution expenses. As of this writing, the maximum contribution an employer can make to a SEP is 15 percent of the employee's wages or $22,500, whichever is less.

Simple to administer and easy to maintain, SEPs have a lot of advantages: whether you're an employee, employer, or both, you don't have to file an annual report with the IRS the way you do with a Keogh, and you can change the amount you contribute annually. (Meaning you can contribute the max during good years and skip payments altogether if things are bad.) If you leave to work somewhere else or find yourself covered by another plan, you can roll your SEP money over into an IRA without incurring any penalty. (However, you can't roll a SEP over into your new employer's retirement plan.)

It can be tricky figuring out the amount you can contribute to a SEP, since for tax purposes your salary (or compensation) isn't based on what you actually earn, but rather on your earnings minus the amount you've put into your SEP. This reduces your actual SEP contribution from 15 percent to 13.04 percent. Those who are self-employed also have to subtract from earnings half the money they've paid out in self-employment tax. Your tax preparer will be able to give you the exact numbers after completing your returns.

IRAs

IRAs, or individual retirement accounts, are retirement plans for individuals who are employed, or for individuals with employed spouses (self-employed people cannot open IRAs). At present, the maximum you're allowed to contribute to an IRA annually is $2,000, or $2,250 in separate, spousal IRAs if you have a nonworking mate. For example, say Chuck and Nora McGinty wanted to open IRAs. They could open two, contributing no more than $1,125 into each annually. You don't need $2,000 to open an IRA; in most cases, a few hundred dollars will do. Once the account is open, you don't have to put money in it every year, although you'll probably want to, since IRAs are one of the best retirement and tax avoidance vehicles around.

In certain respects, IRAs function similarly to some investment plans already mentioned in this chapter. For example, you will have to pay a 10 percent penalty if you try to withdraw money from your IRA before you're 59½, in addition to any taxes that might be due. You must start withdrawing money from your IRA when you're 70½, although you can keep putting away $2,000 a year in a nonworking spouse's plan until he or she reaches that age.

As for your investment options, you're the boss. Your IRA can be invested any way you'd like—a simple savings account, a mix of mutual funds, or individual stocks and bonds. However, keep in mind that trying to keep track of multiple IRAs can be a real headache. For this reason, most people set up all their IRAs in one place, whether it's a bank or a brokerage house. That way, even though you might have many different types of investments, you'll receive a single statement listing them all. Contributions and withdrawals must be reported when you file your tax return.

Since you will have to pay to open and maintain your IRA, or IRAs, it pays to shop around to see which financial institution offers the lowest fees. Some brokerage houses will waive fees depending on how much money is in the account. In general, though, you can expect to pay between $10 and $50 a year to set up and maintain each IRA. This is another reason why you might want to consolidate them.

One of the most frequently asked questions about IRAs is whether the money you put in them is protected. The answer is yes . . . and no. Remember, only deposits of up to $100,000 held in federally insured banks are 100 percent protected. IRAs invested in mutual funds, for example, aren't protected. There are also limits to how much of bank-invested IRAs is protected. Accounts opened before December 19, 1993, are insured up to $100,000 apiece, whether you have one IRA or twenty at the same bank. But accounts opened after that date are insured up to $100,000 in total. This means that if you have recently opened IRAs worth $200,000 in a bank that goes under, the only money you're gonna see is $100,000, period. That's why some people open up each IRA in a different bank. To them, the complexity of keeping track of different IRAs at different institutions is worth the security it provides.

Another drawback: You can't borrow from an IRA the way you can with some pension plans. But you can get at the money during a sixty-day period, once a year, if you withdraw the money, then use it to open a new IRA account with the full amount you withdrew before that period is up. Miss the two-month deadline for reinvestment, however, and it's considered an early withdrawal on which you'll have to pay the penalties plus taxes.

If withdrawing the money and putting the same amount into another IRA account within sixty days sounds like a rollover to you, you're right, it is. But money for IRA rollovers doesn't necessarily need to come for other IRAs. It can come from your company's pension plan, a 401(k), or another type of retirement plan.

Nor do you have to roll your IRA moneys over into the same type account. You can close your savings account–based IRA account (if you have one, please do!), get a check for the amount you've saved, and open up a mutual fund–based IRA account. The only restriction on the rollover is that you must do it within sixty days.

The advantages to an IRA rollover are obvious. First, you can continue to make money on your investment and put off paying taxes until it's time to start withdrawing. And once an IRA rollover is established, you can leave it alone or, if you switch jobs, transfer it into your new company's pension plan.

As is the case with any IRA, the money in the rollover IRA can be invested any way you wish.

The New Roth IRA

New as this book went to press is the Roth IRA. Contributions for this new plan aren't deductible. However, distributions of funds held for more than five years from the date the Roth IRA is set up are *completely* tax free after age 59½, disability or death, or for up to $10,000 of expenses for first time home buyers.

In addition to the tax free distributions, the Roth IRA has other things going for it. You're allowed to withdraw the amount of your regular contributions to the Roth IRA any time, tax free, without having to worry about paying an early withdrawal penalty. Coverage under an employer's pension plan doesn't disqualify you from having a Roth IRA. There are no mandatory distributions during your life, which means you can keep funds in your Roth IRA that will continue to earn additional tax-deferred compound investment returns for as long as you like. Contributions to a Roth can continue after you turn 70½ as well.

Ultimately, the Roth makes the most sense if it contains investments that compound at high rate for a prolonged period of time—such as growth stocks. Why? Because the value of the compounded returns are distributed tax free rather than being taxed at normal rates (which is the case with regular IRAs and other retirement accounts).

SOCIAL SECURITY

Contrary to popular belief, Social Security (which we considered in some detail back in Chapter 2) was not put in place to provide individuals with a retirement income. Rather, it was seen as a service to help those in need. Over the years, however, people somehow came to believe that they were entitled to Social Security, which is why so many retirees pitch a fit when any mention is made of altering federal laws governing this program. (They're entitled to that money, dammit!)

Some pundits say Social Security is viewed as an entitlement because people believe they're getting back the same money they paid into the plan over their working lives. They're not. Today's retirees will collect between 2.5 and 4 times as much as they contributed after adjusting for the interest they would have earned had they invested the money themselves. Today's retirees will collect back all their own contributions after only twenty-one months. A few optimistic souls think that if only the elderly knew these facts they'd be less vehement in opposing reform.

That may or may not be true, but whatever happens, my advice is not to rely on Social Security to fund your retirement. (Most younger folks aren't. In fact, it seems more people believe in UFOs than believe in the continued viability of Social Security.)

That said, I think we can assume that some form of Social Security will be around for as long as it takes for all those who have contributed something to have a chance to collect some benefits. Therefore, it's a good idea to have at least a basic understanding of how the system works.

Simply put, Social Security is there to provide a guaranteed monthly income for those who are retired or disabled, their families, and their survivors should they die. The system is funded by money withheld from your paycheck, as well as the paycheck of everyone else who works.

To qualify for Social Security, you need to have paid your FICA (Federal Insurance Contributions Act) taxes (a worker's share of Social Security taxes, withheld by an employer, or the full amount due, paid along with income tax by the self-employed). You also need to have accumulated 40 "credits" if you were born after 1928. In 1997, a credit was given for every $670 earned. However, no worker garners more than four credits a year, no matter how much money he or she earns. The dollar amount per credit is adjusted every year to reflect cost-of-living increases. So, too, is the maximum income on which you must pay Social Security taxes. It might take you twenty years to get your 40 credits, or it might take you thirty. That doesn't really matter. Once you hit 40 credits, you're in.

The monthly amount you ultimately receive when you retire is currently based on what you've earned during most of your working life, specifically your highest-paying thirty-five years. Up to a point, the more money you've made over the course of your career, the more you'll get. If you've paid the maximum amount of FICA each year and you wait until you reach full retirement age before you begin collecting, you'll be "entitled" to the largest benefit SS gives.

If you're curious about how many credits you have left to go or how much you've paid into the system, you can call 1-800-772-1213 and get a Request for Personal Earnings and Benefit Estimate Statement. After filling out the form, you return it to the Social Security Administration, or SSA. They, in turn, will send you an estimate of what you can expect to receive monthly, based on your age and earnings.

You can start collecting Social Security when you're as young as 62. However, if you do, the amount you receive will be smaller than if you waited until you were 65, when you're eligible for full benefits.

Those between ages 62 and 65 can work while collecting Social Security, but there are some restrictions: in 1997 they could only earn up to $8,640 without affecting their benefits. After that, for every $2 they earn, $1 in benefits would be withheld. For example, let's say you were 63 in 1997, you're collecting Social Security, but you're also working at a job that pays $10,000 a year. You're therefore earning $1,360 too much ($10,000 minus $8,640 equals $1,360). Divide that number by 2 (since Social Security is going to take $1 for every $2 you've earned), and you can see that your Social Security benefits will be reduced by $680 a year.

If you were between 65 and 69 in 1997 you could earn up to $13,500 without hurting your benefits, but for every $3 you earned, SSA would withhold $1. That means that if you're 67 and earning $15,000, you're $1,500 over Social Security's limit, which means your benefit will be reduced by $500 (or one-third of $1,500). Remember, in this age range, Social Security only robs you of $1 out of every $3. As mentioned earlier, these exemptions change so you need to speak with your local Social Security office to get the most up-to-date figures.

Once you hit 70, you're home free: you can collect the full amount of Social Security and make as much money as you would like.

Once you qualify for SS benefits, you'll get them for as long as you live. In addition, your spouse stands to collect as well. As it now stands, spouses are eligible to collect 100 percent of a deceased partner's full retirement benefit at age 65. A surviving spouse can switch from collecting his or her own Social Security benefit to collecting as a survivor if it means he or she is eligible for a larger benefit. (You can't collect both.)

As for the current law on taxing benefits, it's pretty straightforward:

•If you're single, receiving benefits, and your income level is between $25,000 and $34,000, 50 percent of your benefit is taxable. If you make over $34,000, 85 percent of your benefit is taxable.

•If you're married but living apart and filing separate returns, it's the same as above.

•If you're married, living together, and your joint income is between $32,000 and $44,000, 50 percent of your benefit is taxable. Earn above $44,000 and 85 percent of your benefit will be taxed.

That concludes your education on pensions and other retirement plans—but your financial education has just begun. As I've noted, one of the secrets to making the most of your pension contributions (and those of your employer) is to invest those moneys wisely. And one of the secrets to fulfilling your

retirement dreams is to save and invest money above and beyond what's in your pensions. So the obvious question is,
Where do you invest all those dollars? There's no simple answer, but the good news is that you can start figuring things
out by turning to the next chapter.

9

INVESTMENT INSTRUMENTS: THE BUILDING BLOCKS

Pop quiz: What's a Keogh? What's an IRA? After reading the previous chapter, you should be well acquainted with the different kinds of pension plans available. The next step in your retirement education is familiarizing yourself with the many investment instruments available so you can make the most of those plans. But before we address that, a few words about the concept of investing.

RISK VERSUS REWARD

Frightening as the thought may be, there's no such thing as risk-free investing. Every investment that offers a return, or reward, carries some degree of risk. The key word to focus on is "degree." The real issue is the degree or amount of risk you, as an individual, are willing to assume. Put two individuals in the same room, and chances are they'll disagree about which investment instruments are risky.

There are certain immutable laws in the universe. For instance, water always runs downhill, and the Chicago Cubs will never win the World Series. In the financial cosmos, the immutable law states that the greater the potential reward from an investment, the greater the risk, and conversely the lower the potential risk, the lower the reward.

To keep matters simple and as easy to understand as possible, the investments we'll be exploring in this book have been divided among three chapters. In this chapter we'll deal with the most basic investment instruments available. In Chapter 10 we'll explore mutual funds, the best tool available to the individual investor. Finally, in Chapter 11 we'll explore some less common but potentially valuable investment options.

It's helpful to keep in mind that all the investment instruments outlined in these three chapters are what are known as money products. Some can make you heaps of money, others won't. Picking and choosing the right investments for you depends on your personal preference and risk/reward analysis. Some people like to use all high-risk/high-reward tools, some all low-risk/low-reward; others mix and match. (I'll offer you what I think is the best formula for mixing and matching risks and rewards in Chapter 12.) But in order to make an intelligent decision, you need to know how the investment instruments operate, how they differ, and what they have to offer.

CERTIFICATES OF DEPOSIT (CDs)

Low-yielding, interest-paying investment tools, certificates of deposit, or CDs, are considered extremely conservative investments, a mere step above your basic money in, money out savings account. Still, CDs are extremely popular, and it's not hard to understand why: they're easy to open, they're safe (federally insured up to $100,000), and like bonds, they're available in a range of maturities, from one, two, three, six, and twelve months to two and one-half, five, and ten years.

Capitalizing on interest rate movement

If interest rates fall after you've taken out a long-term CD at an earlier, higher interest rate, you're safe. If, on the other hand, rates rise and you're stuck with a long-term CD paying a rate lower than what's currently available, the solution is often to cash in the now underperforming CD, pay the early withdrawal penalty, and take out a new higher-interest CD.

Laddering CDs

Many investors in CDs, especially those who prefer shorter-term investments, often use a technique known as laddering. When you ladder, you pick a variety of CDs with different maturity dates, dividing your money equally among them. As each CD comes due, you reinvest the final amount.

In this way, if interest rates fall as one of your CDs matures, only part of your total CD investment will be reinvested at the current lower rate. The reasoning behind this strategy is that there's a chance that by the time the next CD matures, interest rates will have climbed back up again.

Laddering is a good way to protect yourself against investing all your money when rates are low. Laddering can also be used to generate income. As each CD comes due, you have the option of shifting the money into accounts used for living expenses.

BONDS

Bonds are loans to either corporations or governments. How do they work? By providing you, the investor, with interest payments, which you'll receive from the time the bond is purchased until it matures or is sold (whichever comes first). At that point, you receive back the face value of the bond. The interest you earn may be taxable or not.

As of this writing, the income from corporate bonds can be taxed whereas the income from most municipal bonds is tax free in one form or another (free from either local, state, or federal taxes, or some combination of the three). Moneys invested in U.S. Treasury securities aren't exempt from federal taxes, but are exempt from state and local taxes.

If you're a conservative investor, bonds might appeal to you, as they offer regular, fixed-interest payments until the bond matures, not to mention the face value of the bond when it comes due. Once you get that principal back, it's yours to reinvest.

While investing in bonds is generally considered less chancy than investing in stocks, there are some risks involved; these are related to the length of time until the bond matures; fluctuating interest rates, which can affect bond prices; who you've lent your money to, which affects the quality of the bond; and last but not least, credit, or how you'll fare in terms of getting your money back, whether it be the principal or interest.

A few words on zero coupon bonds

Many investors looking toward the long term invest in what are known as zero coupon bonds. These are bonds that don't pay you any interest income and are therefore sold at less than their face value. When the bond matures, you receive the full amount (face value) of the bond.

For example, if I know that I'll need $5,000 in twenty years I could buy a zero coupon bond with a face value of $5,000 payable in twenty years for, let's say, $3,500. While I'd get no interest during the next twenty years I'd be certain to get exactly the amount I needed when I needed it. As you may have figured out, this is what has made zero coupon bonds very popular among those saving for a child's college tuition.

Why are they called zero coupon bonds? Well, bonds take the tangible form of a document containing a main body and a bunch of coupons. The main body represents the face value of the investment. Each individual coupon represents an interest payment. A zero coupon bond is one that has had all the interest coupons removed. The bond and the interest coupons are sold separately to different individuals or institutions. The person holding the bond itself gets only the face value on maturity. The person holding the interest coupons gets to cash them in for the interest payments.

Like other bonds, zero coupon bonds can be issued by either

the federal, state, or local government, a municipality, or a corporation, and can be tax free or taxable depending upon their status.

Bond Mutual Funds

While mutual funds are dealt with later in Chapter 10, bond mutual funds are worth a brief mention. Bond mutual funds *do not* act like individual bonds. Individual bonds can be held on to until they mature or until they're "called," at which time you get back all the money you've invested. But mutual funds don't mature; they're subject to the fluctuations of the stock market, and the money you get when you sell your shares depends on what shape the market is in at the time. For this reason, conservative investors prefer purchasing individual bonds rather than bond mutual funds. But if you're someone interested in being able to invest in bonds and diversify with only small amounts of money, bond funds might be for you.

Bond Ratings

To ensure quality control, most bonds are related. While there are a number of rating systems, the most commonly used ratings are AAA, AA, A, and BAA bonds.

AAA bonds are those of the highest quality: they carry little risk, and the issuers are known to be stable as well as dependable.

Next best are *AA bonds*. These too are high-quality, but they carry a slightly higher degree of risk than AAA bonds.

A bonds are of high-to-medium quality, but are extremely vulnerable to market conditions.

BAA bonds are good for the short term, but do not perform well over the long haul. They're generally considered to be medium-quality bonds.

Any bond rated lower than BAA is considered to be of poor quality.

It's also possible for a bond to be classified as nonrated, or

NR. *NR bonds* often offer investors higher returns that AAA-rated bonds, but are riskier than even the lowest-rated bond.

Getting the most bang for your bond

Since there are so many types of bonds out there, each with its own advantages and disadvantages, you would do well to gather info on the following before investing.

• Get the full name of whoever is issuing the bond. If it's a new issue, rather than a refinance, get the full details on how and where the money you've invested in your purchase will be spent.
• Find out when the bond's maturity date is—that is, the day in the future when you will be paid the face value of the bond.
• Make sure you're clear on what kind of bond it is: federal or state government, municipal or corporate.
• Ask if the bond is rated, and if so, what its most recent rating is.
• Find out whether the income you receive from the bond will be taxable or not.
• See if the bond is "callable." That means the issuer has the right to redeem the bond early, and not continue to pay the interest. Obviously if a bond is paying above market interest rates and is callable, the issuer will want to pay off its loan (by paying out the face value of the bonds issued) and refinance at the new, lower rates.
• Be clear on the bond's price and face value (that is, the amount the bond will be worth when it hits maturity).

Treasury bills

Treasury bills, also called T-bills, are short-term investment bonds, issued by the federal government, that usually mature in three months, six months, or one year. In most cases, they're used by the government to raise money for immediate spending at significantly lower interest rates than most bonds. They ain't cheap: the minimum investment—make sure you're sitting, now—is generally $10,000.

Treasury bills can be a little confusing, but let me use an oversimplification to explain how they work. Let's imagine you send the government a certified check for $10,000 for a treasury bill due to mature in one year. The government then sends you a check for $1,000. When your bill matures in a year, you'll get another check from Uncle Sam for $10,000 (or the face value of the bill)—meaning that the $1,000 you got when you first bought the T-bill was pure profit. While that's not literally the way the investment transpires, it does explain how you make money buying treasury bills.

Considered a risk-free investment (I know, I know—I said there was no such thing as a risk-free investment. I lied.), treasury bills are exempt from state and local taxes. It's also possible to defer taxes: if you buy a T-bill that's due to mature in the next calendar year, the income interest you earn (even though you get the $1,000 profit right away) can be paid then.

STOCKS

One of the best ways to grow your money over the long term—if not the best way—is by investing in stocks. There are two distinct advantages stocks have over other investment vehicles. One, some stocks pay dividends, which means they will provide you with an income. Two, stocks have historically proven to provide real growth over the long term. If you look at the stock market over a short period of time, there's no denying the market fluctuates, sometimes wildly. But if you look at it over a long period of time, you'll see stock values usually rise. (In fact, overall, stocks rise in value faster than any other form of investment.) This is why stocks are excellent inflation beaters.

A stock represents a share in ownership in a business or corporation. If you own stock, you become a shareholder, which means you own a small part of that business or corporation.

The interest you hold in the company is known as equity. (This is why you'll sometimes hear stockholders referred to as equity investors.)

Income versus growth and common versus preferred

Stocks usually belong to one of two families: *income stocks,* those that pay their shareholders dividends, even if it's at the expense of growing in value; and *growth stocks,* those that don't expect to offer dividends, but instead concentrate on growing in value.

All stocks can also be divided into common and preferred stocks. Usually, the dividends on *preferred stocks* are fixed, so they offer a more regular rate of return than *common stocks,* whose dividends are not fixed.

And here are three other labels commonly attached to groups of stocks: *Value stocks* are stocks considered to be priced at less than the real worth of the company offering them. *Multinational stocks* are shares in companies that have facilities in both the United States and other countries. *International stocks* are stocks in foreign-owned and -based companies.

Buying stocks

As with buying bonds, there are two ways of investing in stocks: you can buy them individually, or you can buy them through a mutual fund. (More on mutual funds in the next chapter.) Whichever route you choose, make sure you find out the following before you buy:

• The name of the company or corporation you'd like to invest in.
• The quality of the management.
• Which stock exchange(s) it trades on.
• Whether the stock pays a dividend or not. If it does, find out how much the dividend is and whether the dividends have gone up or down over time. Stocks that pay regular dividends are good if your goal is generating income. But if your concern

is long-term growth, dividend-paying stocks may not be the way to go.

• How actively the stock is traded. Stocks that are heavily traded are subject to great fluctuations in value.

• Whether the company you're interested in buying stocks in offers a dividend reinvestment plan. This is an easy way for long-term investors to continually acquire company stock.

MORTGAGE-BACKED SECURITIES

Ever hear someone mention Ginnie Maes, Freddie Macs, or Fannie Maes and wonder who those folks were? Actually you were hearing the names of the three most common types of mortgage-backed securities.

Mortgage-backed securities are "pooled" home mortgages. Banks as well as other savings and loan institutions make mortgage loans, which they then "pool" together. Units in this pool are sold to investors, who receive payments (otherwise known as distributions) of both interest and principal as the loans are paid off.

Any pool of mortgages that provides its investors with periodic payment is known as a pass-through. Generally speaking, most mortgage-backed securities are issued by federal agencies, although some private institutions offer them as well. As mentioned above, the three most common are obtained through:

• The Government National Mortgage Association (GNMA, or "Ginnie Mae")
• The Federal Home Loan Mortgage Corporation (FHLMC, or "Freddie Mac")
• The Federal National Mortgage Association (FNMA, or "Fannie Mae")

Most average Joes and Josephines can't afford to invest in them, since they often require a large amount of money up front (we're talkin' $20,000 to $25,000, in some cases). The exception is Ginnie Mae mutual funds, which are within the grasp of most investors (and which are dealt with in the chapter on mutual funds).

Now that we've gone over the major building blocks of investment instruments, let's turn to what I and most other folks think is the best way to assemble a nice collection of these blocks: mutual funds.

10

INVESTMENT INSTRUMENTS: YOUR BEST BET— MUTUAL FUNDS

Mutual funds are hot right now, and with good reason: they're directly responsible for making the rewards of the stock market available to all. Mutual funds are investment pools. The fund consists of money from all different types of investors that is then pooled together and invested, by professional fund managers, in different instruments.

Most mutual funds, while concentrating efforts in one area, diversify into other areas so they're not wiped out by problems in one industry, region, or market. Shares in mutual funds can be purchased by thousands of investors, but the choice of what's purchased to constitute the fund is usually the choice of a single individual, or a team of portfolio managers.

Though the ultimate decision of how to invest your money is up to you, I'd strongly advise doing so through mutual funds. Why? Because:

• You're the one in the driver's seat when it comes to how much risk you want to assume. If you like taking chances, you can invest in a high-risk fund. If the thought of losing money makes you queasy, go for a low-risk fund.

There are funds available for every level of risk you can imagine.

• You can diversify, minimizing your risk, even with a small amount of money. This is because your money is pooled with that of hundreds, if not thousands, of other investors. Thus, your purchasing power is much greater than it would be were you investing on your own.

• You don't have to worry about managing the fund; it is done for you. Each fund is managed by a highly qualified individual whose sole job it is to manage the fund.

• The funds are pretty simple to understand, so much so that most people pick their own mutual funds, bypassing financial consultants entirely. I'll explain later how you can pick your own funds, but if I may put in my two cents, I don't advise it. I think it's better to work with a financial planner. (How to choose one is detailed on pages 175–178.)

• There's information available on how the fund has performed in the past, so you'll know what you're getting into.

• It's possible to reinvest whatever dividends and capital gains you earn. So, thanks to compounding, your returns will be higher than if you'd invested in stocks alone.

No two mutual funds are exactly alike. Each comes with its own set of investment objectives. Some invest for growth, others for income, and others strive to achieve both. Some take high risks, while others take low risks. Some have the goal of growing money over a long period of time, while others have the goal of growing it over a short period. Thanks to their popularity, there are hundreds of different types of mutual funds now available to investors. But since one of the aims of this book is making the complex simple, we're going to focus on the three most basic types of mutual funds: stock funds, bond funds, and money market funds.

STOCK FUNDS

Stock mutual funds are those that invest in shares of common stock. It works like this: An investment company takes your money along with that of others and buys shares of common stock. When and if you cash in your shares, they're redeemed by the fund for the net asset value, or NAV, per share. (NAV is explained in greater detail on pages 139–140.)

Because mutual funds deal with purchases on a large scale, they usually pay a lower commission on stock transactions that those who trade individually. They pass the savings on to you. Below are the most common types of stock funds.

Long-term growth funds

These funds seek capital gains from companies that have demonstrated slow, steady continual growth in earnings. Extremely stable, they're good if you're looking for a conservative long-term investment.

Growth-and-income funds

These funds try to deliver what their name promises: both long-term growth and some income, the latter by investing in dividend-producing stocks. They're considered somewhat safer than growth funds, since they don't focus on just one type of stock.

Balanced funds

Balanced funds mix common and preferred stocks with bonds (I know, this technically isn't a pure stock fund—so shoot me) in the hopes of minimizing investment risk. Like long-term growth funds, they're considered stable, and they offer greater diversification.

Aggressive growth funds

Can you say "risky"? These funds aim to make big bucks for investors by investing not only in small companies poised for growth, but also in other speculative stocks. When the market is strong and the economy is humming, these funds outperform other stock funds by a mile. But if the market turns bearish, the worth of the stocks in these funds can plummet perilously.

In general, aggressive growth funds invest in anything that seems like a steal at the time, since their only concern is making money fast. Unfortunately, some funds try to expedite that process by investing in volatile securities as well as trading with borrowed money. These funds rarely pay dividends to shareholders; instead, profits are funneled back into the company to fund expansion.

Sector funds

Most stock funds aim for diversification. Not sector funds: they invest in the stocks of companies in a single industry or geographic area, hoping to capitalize on the rapid price appreciation that sometimes occurs in one area and results in increased profits. The sectors most commonly invested in are utilities, technologies, oil, and financial services. Considered risky precisely because they do lack the safety net diversification provides, these funds also ask investors to function as fortune tellers, trying to anticipate which industries are about to boom. This is known as trying to time the market, and as any knowledgeable and successful investor will tell you, that's awfully hard to do. My advice is to keep it simple, and stick instead with a diversified mutual fund that will grow your money slowly over the long term.

International Funds

These funds invest in stocks traded on foreign stock exchanges, most notably London, Paris, and Tokyo. Their advantage? They offer investors maximum diversity.

Some international funds also invest in foreign bonds, and a few limit their investments to one area or country in the world. As you might imagine, these latter funds (the geographic equivalents of sector funds) tend to be riskier, since they aren't as diversified. Their returns also tend to be contingent on how well the dollar is performing against other currencies.

Index funds

Index funds are the direct opposite of sector funds. Whereas sector funds try to predict the market and beat it, index funds attempt to mimic the market, the belief being that the best way to make money over a long period of time is by simply buying the market as a whole. Index funds take investors' money, then put together a portfolio of stocks that mirror the composition used by one of the leading market indexes, be it Standard & Poor's or Dow Jones. The hope is that the fund will perform exactly as the market does.

Precious metal funds

One of the more risky forms of investment due to lack of diversification and the volatility of the precious metals business, these funds invest in the stocks of gold mining and other precious metal companies.

BOND FUNDS

Bond mutual funds are the flip side of stock mutual funds. Rather than using its pool of money to invest in a variety of stocks, the fund puts the money into a variety of bonds. Below are the major types of mutual bond funds.

Municipal bond funds

These funds invest in intermediate to long-term municipal bonds. Generally used to fund revenue-producing projects such as highways and waterworks, they offer the investor the advantage of tax-free income.

Since tax laws vary from state to state, often a municipal bond fund will invest in the municipalities of a single state its manager knows offers favorable tax laws. The only problem with this is, while the income you receive might be tax free, there's also little diversification in the fund. If the economy of the state in which you've invested goes into a recession, you're screwed. You should also know that some states do tax the income of bonds issued by out-of-state governments. In general, the federal government doesn't tax municipal bonds, unless they've been used to fund nongovernment projects—in which case it does.

Corporate bond funds

These funds invest in the bonds issued by—take a guess—public corporations. The income from these bonds is taxable, not only by some state governments but by the federal government as well.

U.S. government income funds

Extremely low risk because they invest in government notes, federally backed mortgage securities, and treasury bills, these funds are the conservative investor's dream. If most of the fund is invested in mortgage-backed securities issued through the Government National Mortgage Association, they're called Ginnie Maes. But you already know that, having read all about mortgage-backed securities in the previous chapter.

GNMA funds perform reasonably well when interest rates are high. But when rates drop, it can hurt investors, as homeowners like to take advantage of lower rates and either pay off their mortgage or refinance it at a lower rate. While you'll always get your principal back, you'll be reinvesting it at a lower rate—meaning you won't be getting as much money back as you thought you would.

Luckily, the same doesn't apply to funds that invest in treasury bills, which aren't callable, meaning the government can't call the bills in and reissue them at a lower rate. These funds' yields aren't as affected by plummeting interest rates as those of GNMA funds, although GNMAs do tend to offer a better yield than treasury bills when both are issued around the same time. This means that when the economy is stable and doing well, GNMA funds tend to perform better.

MONEY MARKET FUNDS

Money market funds function much like the money market accounts they're named after: for every dollar you put in, you get a dollar back—plus the interest earned on whatever investment the fund makes. Since these funds are extremely low risk, many investors prefer them over stock and bond funds. They carry a disadvantage in that when interest rates are low, the interest you receive is minimal. But they carry a definite perk as well: you're allowed to write checks against the balance of your fund, and in most cases you won't be charged for it (although sometimes there is a per check minimum).

Taxable money market funds invest in short-term government or corporate debt instruments or securities. One of the elements investors find attractive about such funds—in contrast to stock and bond funds—is that you're never in any danger of losing part of your principal. On the other hand, your money is hardly going to grow faster than inflation in these funds—which is why many investors use them solely as a place to put money temporarily while waiting for market conditions to improve. Once that happens, they withdraw their money and invest it in a fund geared toward long-term growth.

Tax-exempt money market funds offer many of the same advantages and disadvantages of taxable money market funds, but with a key difference; they're slightly riskier. Some of the short-term projects these funds invest in have been created solely to meet the short-term needs of tax-exempt money funds. This means the money in these funds is going toward funding short-term debt, which makes them riskier than funds invested in long-term bonds commonly used to fund revenue-producing projects.

Still, these funds do offer nontaxable income, and if you're lucky enough to fall into the 28 percent or 33 percent tax bracket, you could do well.

OPEN-END VERSUS CLOSED-END

Mutual funds can be either open-end or closed-end. In an *open-end fund* there is an unlimited number of shares. In a *closed-end fund* the number of shares is limited.

Most funds are open-ended, so if you have just decided to invest in a particular fund, you could buy shares today. Right now, there are some 5,300 different open-end mutual funds around, all of them with the same purpose in mind: to make money for you, the investor.

Purchasing shares in an open-end fund is pretty straightforward: you can do it through the mutual fund company itself, or through a banker, broker, or financial planner.

When you invest in an open-end mutual fund, you receive a share of the dividends, as well as any profits that might be earned from the sale of securities. You can receive this money in cash or choose to reinvest the money in additional fund shares. Payouts, or distributions, may be paid monthly, quarterly, or annually.

Closed-end mutual funds offer a limited number of shares to investors. Once that fixed number of shares is purchased, that's it—there are no more available. Closed-end funds can be purchased only through a broker, and they tend to be much riskier than open-end funds. They're best known as avenues for buying bonds and making international investments, though all sorts of varieties are available.

There are two ways to gauge what a closed-end mutual fund is worth. One is by checking its net asset value (see the section on NAVs on page 139). The other is finding out the market value of the fund's own shares.

In most cases, closed-end funds are sold at a discount—

that is, they cost less than their NAV. However, it is possible for investors to drive the value of a closed-end fund above the NAV—in which case it's said that the shares are being sold at a premium. You want to avoid shares being sold at a premium, by the way. Why? Because it usually means they're overpriced.

In an open-end fund you make money if the value of the fund's holdings increases or if the fund issues a dividend. With closed-end mutual funds there is an additional way to make money: you might be able to sell your shares for more than you paid for them.

Of course, you can lose money with closed-end mutual funds, too. A discount can deepen, or the NAV can drop. As a matter of fact, both can happen at once—an investor's nightmare.

Most people who have looked at the issue think it's best for the average investor to stick with open-end funds.

OF LOADS AND NAVs

If you've ever thumbed through the financial section of the newspaper or caught an ad for a mutual fund on TV, no doubt you've heard mention of funds that are no-load, front-end-load, and back-end-load. A load is just a fancy name for a sales charge.

If you invest in a mutual fund that carries a *front-end load,* you're required to pay the sales charge at the time you buy shares in the fund.

Back-end loads are charges you pay when you sell the investments.

No-load funds are those that don't have any sales charge.

There are also funds known as *low-load.* That means the fund's sales charge is considered below industry standards.

In addition to wondering what a load was, you might also have wondered about the letters "NAV" that I've been batting around. As I've mentioned, they stand for net asset value, which is the per share price of the mutual fund. NAVs are calculated daily, according to the following formula:

> The net asset value equals the market worth of the fund's total assets, minus its liabilities, divided by the total number of shares outstanding in the fund.

INVESTIGATING INDIVIDUAL MUTUAL FUNDS

With all these (and literally hundreds of other variations too obscure for me to mention) to choose from, shopping for mutual funds has become as daunting a task as shopping for an individual stock. But you can do it if you take your time and shop wisely. Before investing in any mutual fund, you really need to get a handle on:

• The precise name of the fund and what its investment objective is. Make sure its goals are the same as your own.
• What "family" it belongs to, if any (i.e., Fidelity, Dreyfus, Kemper, etc.).
• Where the fund invests its money (i.e., domestic, international, or both).
• What type of investments the fund makes (i.e., stocks versus bonds).
• What the sales charge will be, if any.
• Whether it's front-end-load, back-end-load, or low-load, or no-load.
• How long the fund has been around.
• Who manages it, and how long he or she has been doing so.
• How much of each investment dollar goes to cover the fund's "overhead."

You also need to get a copy of the fund's prospectus and read it, despite the distinct possibility your eyes will glaze over in the process. (I'll be touching on how to read a prospectus in Chapter 14.)

Finally, make sure you're clear on your reasons for wanting to invest in a particular mutual fund, as well as on how long you anticipate owning shares in the fund, and how you expect those shares to perform.

11

INVESTMENT INSTRUMENTS: OTHER OPTIONS

For most people, investing in stocks and bonds via mutual funds is the best and most sensible way to go. But there are other investment options available, and you should know about them. After all, knowledge is power. When your insurance broker tries to get you to invest in a universal life policy, you need to know not only what that is, but also why you should tell him to take a hike. Conversely, the day your tax preparer asks whether you've ever thought of investing in a real estate investment trust, or REIT, you want to know what he's talking about.

Outlined below are some of these other investment options that I think you should at least know about. Please note that futures, options, commodities, and derivatives are not included, since, like most who have studied them, I think these investments have no place in plans designed to help fund retirement. They're simply too volatile and unpredictable.

LIFE INSURANCE

Most people don't think of life insurance as an investment tool, but today it is often being sold as a way to accrue tax-deferred moneys.

There are basically four different types of life insurance policies available: whole life, universal, term, and variable.

Whole life policies

Whole life insurance policies are often called permanent policies. (That's partly in an effort to get those who have bought lower-cost term policies to think they've got only temporary coverage.) A portion of a whole life premium goes toward paying for the death benefit, while another portion goes into an interest-bearing savings account. The premiums paid for these policies remain level and can be made for a specific period of time, or for life.

If you're the one who's insured and you die, the beneficiary (or beneficiaries) you named in your policy will receive a fixed payment determined by when you purchased the policy.

Whole life policies also have a cash value, based on the value of the savings account portion of the policy. This portion can be borrowed against.

Universal life policies

Universal life policies are just like whole life policies with a few twists thrown in. For instance, premiums and death benefits can be flexible, and a variety of investment options may be offered. Benefits can be determined by the market as well as by how much has been paid in premiums each year.

Term life policies

With term life insurance policies you pay a fixed premium for a specific period of time (hence, "term") with a predetermined death benefit. The term is generally from five to fifteen years. Many policies are guaranteed renewable, however, which means that while premiums may climb at the end of the term, you can still buy coverage. Term is a straight insurance product. There's no cash value ever. The only way it pays off is if you die.

Many people, especially the young, opt for term life, since

the premiums are low. That allows them to get a great deal of coverage for a great deal less than in other insurance products. But as someone ages and becomes a higher risk to the insurance company the premiums will rise. Of course the need for insurance protection will probably drop over time with the accumulation of assets and the fulfillment of financial obligations.

Those who advocate term coverage believe the increased premiums can be offset by renewing for lower amounts of coverage. In addition, they believe that individuals can get better yields investing their own savings than those offered by insurance companies with whole or universal life policies. I agree with them.

Shopping for life insurance

Insurance agents command about as much respect as used car salesmen, and with good reason: many shamelessly prey on people's fear. It's not uncommon for these folks to pressure people shopping for life insurance with such scare tactics as "Suppose you die young? You don't want your family to starve/be penniless/lose the house/live on the street, do you?" To save yourself from falling victim to such a slimy sales spiel, make sure you know:

- what needs you expect the policy to meet
- how long the insurance company you plan to deal with has been in business
- what its rating is

Finding a good insurance agent is like finding a good dentist: once you find one you like and can trust, you'll stick with him or her for life. Ask your friends and family members who they use, or interview a variety of agents on your own. Don't work with anyone who makes you feel pressured or implies that the policy you're interested in won't provide for your family. Only you can be the judge of that.

Most insurance companies give policy holders ten days in

which to decide whether they like the policy or not. If you don't, your money will be refunded.

ANNUITIES

Simply put, an annuity is a contract you make with an insurance company. It's sort of like a reverse insurance policy. Instead of you paying the insurance company premiums each month and then your survivor getting a lump sum when you die, you give the company a lump sum of money when you enter into the contract and the company agrees to pay you a specified income for a specified length of time (usually as long as you live).

Deferred annuities

When it comes to retirement investing, most people opt for what is known as a deferred annuity. They work like this: You fork over your money to the insurance company, either in a lump sum or over a period of time. The insurance company invests your money, and then pays out your benefit when you decide you want to collect. Since the payment is deferred, so too are the taxes on investment earnings, allowing the money in them to grow faster. Deferred annuities can either be fixed or variable.

Fixed annuities

Fixed annuities promise a predetermined rate of return, although that rate can be reset over the years. If, heaven forbid, the rates drop dramatically, the earnings projected for your investment can take quite a nosedive. To safeguard against this, most fixed annuities feature a floor—that is, a guaranteed minimum rate. Unfortunately, this rate is rarely any higher than the prevailing savings rate at the time. Since fixed annuities often do not keep pace with inflation, they are considered a more conservative investment than variable annuities.

Variable annuities

Variable annuities put you in control—that is, you're the one deciding how the money is invested. If this sounds similar to a 401(k) plan, you're right. However, the moneys you invest in a variable annuity have already been taxed, which isn't the case with a 401(k). The investment selection also tends to be more limited, usually only mutual funds.

The pros and cons of variable annuities

As with all investment products, there are advantages and disadvantages to deferred annuities.

Some advantages are:

• You're not locked in to one type of plan—you can pick and choose.
• You're not required to start withdrawing after age 70 if you don't want to.
• Your taxes on the income the annuity generates are deferred until you begin collecting.
• You can put in as much money as you please annually.

The major disadvantages are:

• The fees for maintaining deferred annuities can be hair-raisingly high, and this can affect investment growth, especially in the case of variable annuities.
• While your interest income may be tax-deferred, the money you invest is not—repeat, not—tax deductible.
• If you try pulling any money out of these before you're 59½ you'll be penalized.
• When you are taxed on your annuity earnings they will be treated as straight income, which means that if you have the good fortune of being well off, there will probably be little tax advantage in the end.

Deferred annuity payout options

When the time comes to collect on your deferred annuity—and, unfortunately, to cough up the money to pay the taxes you've deferred—you can choose from two methods of payment: lump-sum withdrawal and regular payouts.

With a lump-sum withdrawal, you'll owe all the taxes up front. The smarter choice would be to take the money in regular payouts, where taxes are owed on a portion of each payout you receive, based on the insurance company's calculation.

Immediate annuities

Immediate annuities perform the way they sound: you give a lump sum to an insurance company and they start making monthly payments to you now, instead of later. (The payment isn't really immediate; you don't get the first check for about a month.)

The size of your monthly or quarterly annuity check is based on your age, the size of your investment, and estimates made by the insurance company on how much your investment will earn them. Since your estimated monthly payout will vary from insurance company to insurance company, depending on how much of a profit they want to make on your money, it pays to shop around for the best rate.

The pros and cons of immediate annuities

A lot of people like immediate annuities because they don't have to worry about managing their money themselves—that's handled by the insurance company. Those who like to control things might not enjoy being unable to make decisions on their own investments, especially if the market changes. While by their very nature all insurance companies should be sound, not all of them are. Some have gotten caught up in highly risky investments of their own. It makes sense to check the health of any insurer with which you're investing. Insurance company health is rated by a number of independent firms, including Moody's and Duff & Phelps. Your public library will have books containing the latest insurance company ratings.

Immediate annuities offer a guaranteed monthly income that you cannot outlive, which many retirees find to be a great source of comfort. Since you've already paid taxes on the money used to fund the annuity, and a portion of the income you're receiving is just a reimbursement of that money, some of the income is tax-free.

But there are downsides as well. For one thing, in most cases the annuity contract is irrevocable. That's right: Sign on the dotted line and that's it, there's no going back. If you need the money for an emergency you're out of luck. (However, there are some new products that allow you to take some money out for medical emergencies. Of course this reduces the income you receive.)

You're also responsible for deciding how much money to put into the annuity. Most financial pundits recommend people put no more than 25 percent of their total nest egg in immediate annuities. That's because if the insurance company with which you've signed the contract goes under, you're up the creek. (Again, this is why it pays to shop around and check the insurer's health.)

Last but not least, if you purchase your annuity at a time when interest rates are low, odds are your payments will not keep pace with inflation.

At present, there are three basic types of immediate annuities available:

Joint annuities

These are annuities that are paid over your lifetime as well as the lifetime of your beneficiary, usually your spouse or life partner. Though the monthly payout tends to be smaller, that's because the payments stretch out over a longer period of time.

Single life annuities

These annuities are paid out each month for as long as you're alive. While you might get a nice, juicy sum each month, if you die your survivor gets zip. The annuity stops when you draw your last breath. As you can imagine, this can be problematic if you and your partner have been using the annuity to help meet basic expenses. (By law, one spouse will actually have to sign a waiver if the other wants to buy a single life annuity.)

Life or period-certain annuities

These are payable for either your lifetime or a fixed amount of time. While the monthly payment is less than you'd receive if you opted for a single life plan, the advantage this annuity has going for it is that should you die before the fixed term ends, your survivor will continue receiving monthly payments of the same amount for the rest of the term.

REAL ESTATE INVESTMENT TRUSTS (REITs)

Real estate investments trusts, or REITs, are investment pools that put their money in real estate, such as shopping centers, office complexes and apartment buildings. Small investors are the most common investors in REITs. Like mortgage-backed securities, REITs pool money raised from investors, and invest it in turn in different real estate assets. REITs are publicly traded, which means they're listed on most major stock exchanges.

There are a number of potential reasons for investing in a REIT. For one thing, REITs allow you to become a part owner of several parcels of industrial, commercial, or residential real estate, which you could probably never purchase on your own. For another, they promise capital appreciation, meaning that you stand to make a profit anytime you choose to sell your shares. Of course, if the market turns cautious, you could lose money.

REITs are also easy to invest in, and easy to get out of. Should you want to sell your REIT, all you have to do is call your broker and tell him to sell. That's a lot easier than owning real estate directly and having to endure the possible agony of putting your property on the market.

Last, and probably most important, REITs have tended to perform very well over the long term. REITs are legally required to give their shareholders 95 percent of each year's profits in the form of regular dividend payouts. Assuming the properties in which you've invested remain profitable, this could provide you with a guaranteed source of income.

As of this writing, there are three types of REITs available: equity REITs, mortgage REITs, and hybrid REITs.

Equity REITs

These are REITs that use investors' moneys to snap up income-producing properties—any property that features rent-paying tenants. Equity REITs tend to be the best choice for those who want to produce a stream of income as well as those interested in capital appreciation. (Historically they have appreciated between 4 and 7 percent annually.) Equity REITs are usually inflation beaters, since in most cases real estate values tend to rise over the long term rather than drop. They're good for folks who want a diversified portfolio but don't want the responsibility of doing their own real estate investing (the REIT invests for you, as well as buying and managing the properties involved).

Look for REITs that buy and manage their own properties as well as focus on specific types of real estate or regions. There are REITs that spread their investments across the country as well as mix and match real estate, industrial, and commercial purchases, but you should try to avoid them, since their success rates tend to be lower.

A couple of caveats: You'll never feel comfortable being an investor in a REIT if you can't deal with the prospect of owning part of a piece of property which you've never even seen, or if you're uncomfortable owning the type of property the REIT invests in, whether it's megamalls or hospitals. And be careful that the REIT isn't being used as an exit for a real estate entrepreneur who has made a mistake.

To choose the best equity REIT for you, get a prospectus from the REIT itself or from your broker. Be sure that it's stated somewhere that the REIT has been around—and had been at least moderately profitable—for at least five years. Avoid REITs that pay their investors' dividends by tapping company cash reserves or selling off properties. Look instead to invest in a REIT whose dividends continue to increase and whose moneys are derived from the rental income of the properties cited in the portfolio.

Mortgage REITs

These REITs invest in mortgages on commercial properties and generate their profits by charging interest to the buyers and developers to whom they've lent money. Though their potential yield tends to be higher than that of equity REITs (somewhere between 6 and 10 percent annually), they tend to invest in fewer properties, which means the potential for capital appreciation is significantly lessened.

One big drawback to mortgage REITs is obvious: if the borrowers default or run out of money, the value of your stock in the REIT will fall. Unlike equity REITs, these REITs behave more like bonds than like the real estate market.

Hybrid REITs

These REITs combine qualities of both equity REITs and mortgage REITs: not only do they own property, but they also make loans. While hybrid REITs do promise a higher yield than mortgage REITs, their potential for capital appreciation is less than that of a straightforward equity REIT.

REVERSE MORTGAGES

Reverse mortgages (which I mentioned briefly in Chapter 3)

are a way of tapping the equity in your home for a steady source of income. Here's how they work.

First, a lender (usually a bank) agrees to make you a loan against the value of your house. You may not need to pay anything up front: all closing and insurance costs can be included in the loan. You're also not responsible for paying any interest on the money you borrow. Instead, it accrues and has to be paid when the loan comes due. The loan money is usually paid out in fixed monthly payments rather than in one lump sum.

The amount you'll receive monthly is determined not only by the value of your house but also by your age and the age of your spouse. Those checks can keep coming for as long as you live in the house, or even for your entire lifetime. If the lender eventually pays out more than the value of your house, it cannot come after your estate's other assets—it swallows the loss.

Should you die or decide to move, the loan comes due. If your house is sold, the proceeds from the sale can go toward repayment of the loan and all the accumulated interest. Once again, any shortfall is the bank's problem. (Don't feel bad for them; they'll make sure they don't lose money by not lending you the house's full value.) Any profit could be yours, the bank's, or shared, depending on the terms of the loan.

You don't have to get the money in the form of monthly checks, although most people do. Other options include a lump sum payment, or a line of credit, which allows you to draw as little or as much money as you need.

The beauty of a reverse mortgage is that it allows you to remain in your home while drawing an income that can be put toward anything you wish, whether it's household expenses or medical bills. In addition, the payments you receive don't count as income, so neither your Social Security nor your income tax will be affected.

But no financial tool is without drawbacks, as you must know by now. One of the most obvious drawbacks to reverse mortgages is that they have higher interest rates than traditional mortgage loans. Another minus, which many people fail to take into account, is that if you leave the house, you may end up with zip—no equity with which to invest in a new home. And, of course, if the house is sold upon your death to pay the loan it cannot be passed on to your heirs.

Remember that age is a significant factor when it comes to considering reverse mortgages as well. If you're a young retiree, don't expect to receive a whopping check every month. People who go for reverse mortgages tend to be 75 and up.

Last but not least, when opting for a reverse mortgage, you run the risk of hanging on to a home you might be better off letting go, both financially and emotionally. For this reason, make sure you want to stay put in the same house when you retire before even investigating this option.

By now, I'm sure your head is swirling, and minor panic has begun to set in. Okay, you're thinking. I can tell a Keogh from a SEP and I'm hep to why mutual funds are hot and REITs are becoming popular. But how do I put these acronyms together into one nice, tidy investment package that will ensure that the money I need will be there waiting for me when I retire? Easy: Just turn the page.

12

PUTTING IT ALL TOGETHER

If you've come this far, you've figured out a few key issues when it comes to investing for retirement. You know where you are now financially; you know where you want to end up, both physically and financially, when it comes time to retire; you know how much you need to come up with to get there; and you know about the various pensions, retirement plans, and investment instruments you can use on your journey. Your next step is to take action and determine your investment strategy.

As I mentioned in Chapter 7, your strategy will in large part be determined by how much money you need to generate between now and retirement, and how much time you have to generate it. Why? Because those are the main factors that determine how much risk you can assume when investing.

A FEW WORDS OF WISDOM ON INVESTING

It's impossible to develop a sound strategy without knowing a few truths about investing. Proved time and time again over the course of history, these boil down to:

Don't get fancy
There's no need for you to invest in futures and commodities if basic stocks and bonds will do the job.

When thinking long-term growth, stocks are the way to go
As I've pointed out repeatedly, while the stock market might fluctuate over the short term, over the long term stocks have continually proven to rise in value more than any other investment vehicle.

Invest in stocks and bonds through mutual funds
If you're a stockbroker or an expert on the market, feel free to pick stocks and bonds yourself. But assuming you're not, you should leave it to folks who not only know what they're doing, but will also manage your money for you, diversify your investments, and minimize your risk: mutual fund managers.

Invest on a regular basis
Investing money at fixed intervals is the single best way to both save and make money.

First, it's the simplest method. If you've a 401(k) or similar work-related plan, just have the money deducted from your paycheck. If you have your own plan, make the regular investment yourself.

Second, it's the most efficient way to invest. The technique is known as dollar cost averaging, and the idea behind it is to invest the same amount of money at fixed intervals regardless of how the stock market is performing. By doing this (rather than trying to guesstimate the best time to buy, which no one can do), you actually reduce your average cost per share.

Here's how it works. Imagine that you've figured out that you can invest $200 monthly in a growth stock mutual fund. Shares are incredibly cheap that first month, a mere one dollar each, so you invest in 200 shares. Next month, however, prices jump to $2 a share, so you can only buy 100 shares. In two months' time, then, you've spent $400 for 300 shares, which means you've paid roughly $1.33 per share.

But suppose you'd decided you would buy 200 shares a month no matter what they cost. Well, then you would have paid $200 the first month and $400 the second—which averages out to $1.50 per share. Or suppose you'd tried to "time" your purchases. If you'd timed it right, you might have been able to buy 400 shares that first month when they were going for $1 apiece. But suppose you timed it wrong, and wound up buying the shares when they were $2 apiece. As you can see, timed buying is a gamble. That's why regular fixed-amount investing makes the best sense.

Remember the savvy investor's maxim: diversify

Yes, stocks are the way to go for the long term, but you can't forget about the short term, either. For that reason, you need to also invest in products that will protect your money during those years when the market dips. These products, along with your stocks, constitute what's known as your portfolio. Your portfolio is made up of every investment, retirement account, and savings account you own, and it could include the following: your home (which as we know provides equity), stocks, money market mutual funds for more immediate savings, and bonds and maybe even dividend-paying stocks.

Don't let market fluctuations influence your investment plan

Will there be bad years when stock prices will drop and you'll lose money? Yessiree. But that shouldn't send you into a tailspin. Your focus is on long-term growth, remember? So when the market dips, stay calm and focused—and don't touch the money you've invested.

Reinvest dividends

As you now know, not all stocks yield dividends. But if yours do, avoid the temptation to take that found money and run. Instead, reinvest and buy more stocks. You'll never be sorry.

The dreaded C-word

With all this advice about stock purchasing, it would be remiss of me not to address the fear some potential investors harbor about stock market crashes. Yes, the market has crashed before. Will it crash again? No one knows. But even if it does, those drops are only temporary. That's why it's important to hold on to your stocks for decades at a time if you can. History has shown that the longer you hold on, the better your chances of earning compound annual returns that range between 10 and 20 percent. No other investment tool can promise that.

MINIMIZING INVESTMENT RISK

There's no point beating around the bush: There are risks involved in every investment. The time to learn about these risks, and the way to mitigate them, is now—before you start investing.

Inflation risk

This is the risk that investors in bonds and other fixed-income securities fear most, since it can diminish—perhaps even destroy—the purchasing power of capital. You can combat inflation risk by avoiding a portfolio consisting of bonds only, even if you're retired; investing in stocks for growth; and not keeping vast sums of cash in short-term investment products, like money market mutual funds.

Market risk

Market risk is the risk of investing badly and consequently losing your money. To minimize the chances of this happening you should diversify so that if one of the investments in your portfolio drops in value, there will be others to offset the loss.

Interest rate risk

This is the bane of bond investors' existence: interest rates rise, and the value of your bonds (or bond mutual funds) drops. Worse, whatever income you're earning won't beat out taxes and inflation. To help protect against interest rate risk, make sure you invest in bonds that mature in two to ten years. Should rates rise, these bonds don't lose as much value as those due to mature over the long term.

Economic risk

This is the risk we all face when the economy goes south. To offset this risk, don't invest in products that will leave you high and dry (and a helluva lot poorer) during a recession, such as junk bonds and limited partnerships.

Holding-period risk

Holding-period risk is that of having to sell an investment at a point where that investment is worth less than you paid for it. To cut down the chances of this type of risk, plan your investments according to how soon you'll need the funds. For example, if it's ten years before your kids are going to be in college, invest in long-term growth instruments.

Reinvestment risk

This is the risk facing those who invest in CDs, money market mutual funds, and other short-term investment instruments that must be reinvested within a short period of time, and thus are more likely to suffer the effects when interest rates drop. To adjust for such risk, "ladder" your fixed-income investments. (Laddering was explained in some detail on page 123.)

Liquidity risk

An investment is considered liquid if it can be sold immediately (at market price) for the purpose of raising cash. While it's not necessary for all your investments to be liquid, enough of them should be so that there's money available for significant cash outlays you're anticipating, such as regular payment of Junior's college tuition bill. Liquid investments include the following: money market mutual funds (although you may have to pay a penalty if you take the money out early), individual stocks, retirement accounts (again, if you break into them too soon, you're gonna pay), and mutual fund shares. Illiquid investments include real estate and your own business.

Minimizing liquidity risks is simply a matter of balancing liquid and illiquid assets. Most financial advisors suggest having enough liquid assets to carry you for a year.

I'll say it again: There's truly no such thing as a risk-free investment. The key to smart investing is making sure your goals for retirement and the amount of risk you're willing to assume are compatible. Below, some pointers to help you:

• Invest in stocks. Not only do stocks promise long-term growth, they also generate income from dividends and capital gains.

• Don't forget medium- and long-term bonds. Medium-term bonds can add to your income and protect you from deflation. They also add some stability to your stock portfolio. Long-term bonds are the best protection against deflation.

• There's nothing wrong with CDs. Of course, that's providing you're only using them as a quick cash reserve, not as an investment tool.

• Real estate is still a good investment tool. It may never again boom enough to be the primary source of your retirement money—as it might have been for your parents—but it's still likely to outpace inflation, especially if you hang on to it over a long period of time.

ASSET ALLOCATION

At this point you probably understand why you need to invest in stocks and other types of instruments simultaneously. The obvious question, however, is, how do you find the right mix? That mix is called asset allocation and it's important. How you split the assets in your portfolio will have a direct influence on whether you'll have enough money to fund your retirement or not.

As I pointed out when I discussed regular periodic investing, trying to time the market generally leads to losses, not gains. The fact of the matter is that the market behaves unpredictably in the short term. However, it's highly predictable in the long term. That's why the types of assets you hold are much more important than when you buy them. Assets rise and fall in value all the time. That's just the way it is. But by mixing and matching assets that rise and fall at different times, you will minimize your investment risk.

When choosing which assets to own, remember the following:

• No matter what assets you pick, try to own as many as you can via mutual funds.

• Diversity doesn't mean owning ten different stocks or five different bond funds. You have to make different types of investments—both stocks and bonds—for a portfolio to be considered diversified.

• For long-term economic growth (and as a hedge against moderate inflation), you should buy foreign as well as domestic stocks.

• If you need to keep the value of a portfolio very stable, at least 10 percent of it should be invested in short- to medium-term bonds, as well as those financial instruments which can be liquidated quickly (short-term treasury bills, money market mutual funds).

Whatever combination of instruments you wind up buying, pundits say your portfolio should include, at the very least, a mix of U.S. stocks, medium-term bonds, and cash equivalents (like the money market mutual funds mentioned earlier).

ASSET ALLOCATION FORMULAS

Obviously there are an infinite number of ways you can divide up your assets. How you choose to do so depends (as I'm sure you're now tired of hearing) on how much risk you're willing to assume, how much you want to make, and how long you've got to make it.

If you're willing to (and need to) assume high risk, most of your investments should be in stocks. If you're a low-risk kind of chap (or need to keep your money especially safe), investing in bonds and cash will appeal to you. Below are the very simplest asset allocation formulas for high, medium, and low risk.

- *High risk:* invest exclusively in stock mutual funds.
- *Medium risk:* 50 percent of your investment should be in stock mutual funds, 40 percent in bond mutual funds, and 10 percent in money market mutual funds.
- *Low risk:* 50 percent of your investments should be in money market mutual funds, 30 percent should be in bond mutual funds, and 20 percent should be in stock mutual funds.

If both your salary and your investment confidence are low, if the thought of taking risks gives you a major case of the heebie-jeebies, or if you've only got a few years to go before retirement and you seem to be in good shape, a low-risk portfolio might be for you.

If you're young and have time to rebound after a financial loss, earn a lot of money, have a great deal of confidence, or need to make a sizable amount of money in only a few years, look into establishing a high-risk portfolio.

A personalized asset allocation formula

Since those simple asset allocation formulas aren't specific enough for you to actually start investing, I'm going to offer a much more detailed formula. But before I do, let me stress that while this formula represents a widely accepted approach to retirement investing, it's not the only one out there. Everyone needs to develop a personal asset allocation formula based on his or her particular situation and unique circumstances. Use this formula as a starting point for developing your own. That said, let's get into the numbers.

Subtract your current age from 100. If you're married, use the age of whoever is older, unless the timing of your retirement is tied to the cessation of work for one particular partner, in which case that person's age should be used. Whatever number you come up with, that percentage of your portfolio should be invested in equities. For example, I'm 36 and my husband is 40. Based on this formula, 60 percent of our assets should be invested in equities. But don't stop there. If you plan on retiring early, add another 10 percent to the amount invested in equities; do the same if you're going to invest through a mutual fund. Since my husband and I do invest through mutual funds, but we're not planning on retiring early, we should have 70 percent of our savings in equities.

As I mentioned earlier, I recommend that all your investing should be done via mutual funds. But what kind should you use for the equity portion of your portfolio? That depends on your age/risk analysis. A moderate approach would be to take 40 percent of your equity money and put it into long-term growth or index funds, put another 40 percent of your equity money into aggressive growth or sector funds, and the remaining 20 percent of your equity money in international funds.

The debt portion of your portfolio—that percentage not invested in equities—should be invested in bond mutual funds: two-thirds invested in municipal or corporate bond funds, and the remaining one-third in U.S. government bond funds.

Your asset allocation formula cannot be carved in stone. Over the years, as you get older, as your personal circumstances change, and as your ability to recover from risks decreases, you need to slowly shift your assets from equities to debt instruments. Of course, this also depends on the time you've got between now and retirement, as well as what your goals in retirement are. A good general rule, however, is to take half the money you shift from equity to debt as you get older, and put it into cash instruments like money market mutual funds. The other half can go into bond funds.

Obviously you'll need to tinker with this formula to suit your personal wants and needs. Let's say you're someone who wants or needs to invest more aggressively than the formula allows. You can do all or some of the following:

• Invest a higher percentage of your money in equities—say jumping the number another 5 or 10 percent.
• Put a higher percentage of your equity money into aggressive growth or sector funds—perhaps increasing it up to 50 or 60 percent.
• Put a higher percentage of your equity money into international funds—maybe investing as much as 40 percent of your equity money overseas.
• Put less of the money you transfer from equity as you age into cash—perhaps avoiding money market mutual funds entirely, just sticking with bond funds.

On the other hand, if you're someone who needs or wants more security, you could do one or more of the following:

• Invest less of your money in equities—perhaps decreasing the amount by 5 or 10 percent.
• Invest a larger share of your equity money in long-term growth or index funds—maybe eliminating the agressive growth and sector fund investments entirely.
• Invest less of your money in international funds—perhaps putting only 10 percent of your money overseas.
• As you age and transfer money from equity to debt, invest more in money market funds than bond funds—maybe putting 60 or 70 percent of those transfers into cash equivalents, rather than just 50 percent.

Whatever the composition of your portfolio, do not—I repeat, do not—obsess on it with every fluctuation of the market. You'll only drive yourself and everyone around you crazy. I suggest you pay attention to the market in general all the time, but only focus on your personal portfolio once, or at most twice, a year. Most people reassess their portfolios annually, usually at tax time, when they have all their numbers on the kitchen table and when they're figuring out how much they can invest in their pension plans. I recommend that after you have your investment portfolio established, you do the same.

So there you have it: all the tips and strategies a neophyte investor needs to get started. I could wish you luck, bid you adieu, and end the book here. But being a kindhearted woman, I won't. Instead, in order to make applying all the rules and formulas easier, I'll show you how it was done by the Harpers, the Kahns, and the McGintys.

13

INVESTMENT STRATEGIES

L et's take a look at how our three couples applied the asset allocation formula I outlined in the previous chapter.

The Harpers, you may recall, plan to leave Boston and move to Bennington, where Tim, having taken an early retirement from his law practice, will pursue freelance writing. Right now, Tim and Sarah have $1,000 in a savings account; $4,000 in a checking account, which they use to pay the bills; $2,000 in a growth-and-income mutual fund; and $5,000 in another growth-and-income stock mutual fund through Sarah's 401(k) at work. They also have $2,500 in a ninety-day CD, and a life insurance policy with a cash value of $750. Their condo is worth $300,000, and their combined income is $135,000. Right now, they're managing to save $10,000 a year, every penny of which they're going to need, since the projected annual income they'll need in retirement is $93,750—or $196,875 a year if you factor in inflation.

The first step the Harpers need to take to get their financial house in order is to take the $1,000 they have in an unproductive savings account and combine it with the money they have in their current CD into another ninety-day CD. This money is going to serve as their emergency cash reserve.

Next, they need to investigate whether it would benefit them to cash in their life insurance policy. As it turns out, the answer is yes: opting for term life policies frees them up to take the $750 they get from cashing in their whole life policy and putting it in the same ninety-day CD mentioned above.

Now it's time for Tim and Sarah to use the asset allocation formula to figure out what their investment portfolio should look like. Tim's yen for early retirement, plus the fact that the Harpers will be investing through mutual funds, adds an additional 20 percent to the figure we get when we subtract Tim's age, 38, from 100. This means roughly 85% of the Harpers' money should be invested in equities, 15 percent in debt instruments. To get the ball rolling. Sarah takes the $5,000 in her 401(k) currently invested in a growth-and-income fund and reallocates it by putting $2,500 into an aggressive growth fund, and $2,500 in a long-term growth fund. They also take the $2,000 they have invested on their own in a growth-and-income fund and instead put it into an international fund.

The Harpers are ahead of the game since they're already saving $10,000 a year, but they could probably afford to save more. After a careful perusal of expenses, Tim suggests Sarah stop giving money to NPR and Planned Parenthood. Sarah refuses, pointing out that these causes are very important to her, and besides, she and Tim get a charitable contribution tax deduction for giving. Tim backs down. Going back over their books, the Harpers discover they spend $2,000 a year on compact discs, videos, and books. Sarah posits they could probably cut the figure in half if they used the library and rented videos instead. Tim agrees, giving the Harpers another $1,000 to invest.

The money the Harpers save over the course of the year should be allowed to accumulate in a money market fund. Since they already have $7,000 invested in equities, they decide to take $1,200 of their annual savings and invest it in debt instruments to give their existing portfolio balance of it—$800—two-thirds is invested in a corporate bond fund; the remaining $400 goes into a U.S. government bond fund.

As I'm sure you've noticed, Tim and Sarah still have $9,800 to play with. Using their personalized asset allocation formula, they decide to put roughly 85 percent—or $8,300—in equities. That money is further broken down according to the formula: 40 percent—or $3,320—in their long-term growth fund; 40 percent—or $3,320—in their aggressive growth fund; and the remaining 20 percent—or $1,660—in their international fund. This leaves the Harpers with $1,500 to invest in debt instruments. They put $1,000 (two-thirds) in their corporate bond fund, and $500 in their U.S. government bond fund. In order to get the most tax benefit, they put as much of this money as possible in Sarah's 401(k) and a new IRA they open for Tim.

The following year, the Harpers again save $11,000. But this time, since their original need to balance their initial portfolio is satisfied, they can instead apply the formula to the entire $11,000, meaning $9,350—or 85 percent of it—can go into equities. (I'm sure you know this breakdown by heart by now, but a little repetition won't kill you.) Of that, 40 percent—or $3,740—goes into their long-term growth fund; another 40 percent—$3,740—goes into their aggressive growth fund; the remaining 20 percent—or $1,870—is placed in their international fund.

As for the $1,650 left to invest in debt instruments, $1,100 (two-thirds) goes into their corporate bond fund; the remainder—$550—goes into their U.S. government bond fund.

Once again, as much of this investing as possible is done through Sarah's 401(k) and another new IRA for Tim.

When the third year for investing rolls around, the Harpers, like the Kahns, should reassess both the investments in their portfolio and their asset allocation formula.

THE KAHNS

As you'll recall, Mitch and Sheryl are 46 and 49, respectively, and their goal is to be able to move to a retirement community in Florida when Mitch hits 65. This means they've got fifteen years in which to save, which is good, especially when you consider that daughter Missy is still in college and they're shouldering that financial burden.

Right now, the Kahns combined income is $100,000. As we learned earlier, they have $2,500 in a savings account, $4,000 in a checking account from which they pay their bills, $8,000 invested in a growth-and-income mutual fund through Sheryl's 401(k) at work, and a $250 savings bond from Mother Kahn. Their house is worth $125,000. They've figured they will need $75,000 a year to live on in retirement. With inflation, that figure rises to $172,500 a year.

The first thing the Kahns need to do is cash in that low-earning savings bond and add the money to their savings account. The grand total? $2,750. But rather than let that money sit in a savings account earning *bupkis,* they should put it into a ninety-day CD account that earns a bit more and yet still provides some liquidity. This will be their emergency cash reserve. Granted, it's not much, but it's better than nothing, and while they acknowledge it's going to be a pain in the *tuchis* rolling it over every three months, they also know the interest they'll be accruing is found money. Plus, they can get at the money in a hurry if they need to—which, God willing, they won't.

The next thing that needs to be done falls to Sheryl. Right now, the money in her 401(k) at work is invested very conservatively. The next time she's able to redirect the $8,000 that's currently there, she should take 40 percent of it—or $3,200—and invest it in a long-term growth mutual fund; another 40 percent—or $3,200—should be invested in an aggressive growth mutual fund, and the remaining 20 percent—or $1,600—should go into an international mutual fund.

Once that's taken care of, it's time for the Kahns to apply the asset allocation formula provided in the last chapter to establish a starting point from which to develop their investment portfolio. Since the timing of their retirement is contingent on Mitch's age rather than Sheryl's, we subtract his age, 46, from 100, and get 54. But don't forget: Since the Kahns plan on investing through mutual funds, they add another ten to that number, bringing it to 64. The Kahns now have the needed investment guidelines: 64 percent of their savings should be in equities, and 36 percent (the remainder) in debt instruments. Of the money being invested in equities, 40 percent should be invested in a long-term growth mutual fund, 40 percent in an aggressive growth mutual fund, and 20 percent in international funds—the same breakdown they've applied to Sheryl's existing 401(k) funds. Since Mitch is under 50, the remaining 36 percent of their savings should be invested entirely in bond funds.

Of course, their investment portfolio is little more than pie in the sky unless the Kahns figure out a way to cut expenses to come up with the money with which to invest. Going over their expenses, they see that they're now spending about $2,400 a year on dining out with friends and seeing first-run movies. After much deliberation, Mitch and Sheryl figure they can save at least $1,200 a year simply by spending more time at Blockbuster Video and less time at their favorite French restaurant.

Another area where they could stand to trim the fat is personal grooming, which is costing them $2,520 a year. While neither of them can forego haircuts, Mitch wonders if it's really necessary for Sheryl to get her nails done every week to the tune of $1,560 a year. He points out that if she has them done only once a month, it would only cost them $360 a year, leaving them with a savings of $1,200 which they could use to invest.

Sheryl reluctantly agrees to cut back her trips to Adele's House of Nails—but only if Mitch is willing to make a personal sacrifice as well. Mitch knows his golf club membership, combined with his addiction to golf gadgets, costs the family about $1,800 a year. Though it's like a knife through his heart, he agrees not to renew his club membership, opting to tee off on a public course instead. He also promises he'll buy just one golf goody a year on his birthday. Total savings? $1,000.

While sitting at their kitchen table figuring all this out, the mail arrives, and with it notification that it's time for their temple's annual pledge drive. Mitch grumbles about shelling out the usual $1,000 donation, until Sheryl points out that they hardly ever go to temple anymore. She suggests they could get a reduced membership, now that Missy's at college and both kids are out of Hebrew school. Mitch agrees, promising to investigate whether they can simply buy tickets for the family to attend temple on the High Holy days and leave it at that. The amount they anticipate saving? $500.

If the Kahns indeed manage to cut back in all the ways outlined above, at the end of a year they should have $3,900 to invest. But that money isn't going to just magically appear; it'll be coming in bits and pieces over the course of twelve months. What the Kahns need to do is open a separate money market account to stash that money away in. The reason? If they put it in checking, they'll wind up spending it.

Flash-forward to one year later. Though the president of their temple is a bit upset, and Sheryl's nails aren't the work of art they once were, the Kahns have achieved their goal: they've managed to save $3,900. Now it's investment decision time. Since they already have $8,000 invested in equities through Sheryl's 401(k) they decide to invest all the $3,900 in a bond mutual fund to come close to, the approximate 64/36 balance they're looking for. Of that $3,900, they put two-thirds—or $2,600—in a corporate bond fund, and the remaining $1,300 in a U.S. government bond fund. In order to take maximum advantage of the tax deferral available to them, as much of this money as possible is invested through Sheryl's 401(k) and an IRA that Mitch has established.

The following year, the Kahns manage once again to save $3,900. Using their personalized asset allocation formula, the Kahns take $2,500 of that money and invest it in equities, breaking it down as follows: $1,000 in an aggressive growth fund, $1,000 in a long-term growth fund, and $500 in an international fund. They are now left with $1,400 to invest in debt instruments, and they allocate it as follows: $933 in a corporate bond fund, and $467 in a U.S. government bond fund. Once again, they use Sheryl's 401(k) and Mitch's IRAs to maximum advantage.

As you can see, it took the Kahns a year to marshal the funds needed to balance their existing portfolio. They followed the same asset allocation formula for a second year as well. But when it comes time to invest for the third year, they may want to reassess their asset allocation formula.

THE McGINTYS

Of all our couples, Chuck and Nora McGinty are in the worst financial shape. Right now, they have $300 in a savings account, $2,000 in a checking account, and a $300 savings bond. Chuck earns $60,000 a year. Their house is worth $225,000.

You may recall that Chuck and Nora figured out that in retirement they would need $45,000 a year to live on—or $54,000 in inflated dollars. Chuck's pension will provide them with $35,000 a year. But since they're hellbent on staying on Long Island, they're going to need to figure out a way to come up with the additional $19,000 through investments, Social Security, and working.

Before we even get into the issue of investing, let's take a look at some changes Chuck and Nora need to make right now. First, they need to cash in their savings bond and add the money to their savings account, bringing the total there to $600. They should then take that money and put it in a better-earning yet just as accessible money market fund.

Nineteen thousand dollars ain't small potatoes, and since the McGintys live frugally as it is, there is simply no room for them to make cuts in their budget in order to begin saving money. The only option open to them then is to bring in more income. Since Nora never went to college and hasn't worked outside the home since their marriage, her marketable skills are few. Still, she gets a job as a cashier at a major drugstore chain. Her full-time salary? Fifteen thousand dollars a year. After taxes and expenses she can put away $10,000.

Since the McGintys are getting by just fine right now on Chuck's salary, they decide that Nora's entire salary will go into a money market fund. At the end of a year's time, obviously, the McGintys have $10,000 with which to invest. Using the asset allocation formula, we subtract Chuck's age, 60, from 100. The result? Forty percent of the McGintys' money—or $4,000—will go into equities. The remaining 60 percent—or $6,000—will be invested in debt instruments.

Unlike the Kahns and the Harpers, the McGintys do not have time on their side. They need to grow money quickly, but to do so would require investing aggressively. This would mean a greater risk of financial loss, which the McGintys simply can't afford at this stage in their lives. Needing to play it safe, they decide to invest the entirety of their $4,000 in a growth-and-income mutual fund, a conservative choice. As for the $6,000 they have to put in debt instruments, they also go the conservative route, $4,000 invested in a municipal bond fund, and $2,000 in a U.S. government bond fund.

For the next five years, this is how the McGintys invest, using the money Nora earns, and putting as much of it as possible into IRAs for both of them. By the time Chuck is ready to retire, they will have $50,000 in investments, plus accumulated interest and earnings. Unfortunately, this is likely to give them only about $3,000 a year in additional income, and that's if they're lucky. Though this, coupled with Chuck's Social Security will help take a small bite out of the $24,000 gap they need covered, it's not nearly enough. What are the McGintys going to do?

The first thought that comes to mind is to move. Many of their friends have headed for the Sun Belt, where they seem to be living quite well on a fraction of what it costs to live in the

New York metropolitan area. But Chuck and Nora are stubborn: they really, truly want to stay right where they are. To do that Chuck will have to keep working full-time, and so will Nora. Both are willing. Of course, they'll have to weigh how much they can earn against how much they're foregoing in Social Security benefits by working. But there is something that can help ease their financial burden somewhat: a reverse mortgage. By the time Chuck retires their house will be paid up. By taking out a reverse mortgage against the value of their house, the McGintys will have yet another source of income. While they would prefer to pass their home on to their children, they're probably not going to have that luxury.

Right about now, I'm sure you're thinking that's all very well and good for the Harpers, Kahns, or McGintys. But how are *you* supposed to pick funds and decide where to invest your money?

Take your finger off the panic button and relax. As fate would have it, investment tactics just happens to be the subject of our next chapter.

14

INVESTMENT TACTICS

You now know all about the different types of mutual funds. You've got an asset allocation formula that will help you see what your investment portfolio should look like. You're ready to roll, right? Wrong. No matter how financially savvy you are, picking the specific mutual funds, stocks, bonds, and other instruments that can make up your retirement fund can be a time-consuming, not to mention incredibly daunting, task. That's why there's one more step I think you need to take: hire a financial planner.

No offense, but financial planners are, in all likelihood, much more skilled at selecting investment products than you'll ever be. This is a person who won't just tell you to invest in aggressive mutual funds; he or she can tell you which aggressive funds you should invest in—and why.

Financial planners can also provide an unbiased opinion on any investment decisions you've made on your own up to this point, as well as make suggestions that can help you better grow your money.

CHOOSING A FINANCIAL PLANNER

Unfortunately, almost anybody can claim to be a financial planner, from your insurance agent to your Uncle Elroy who works part-time for H & R Block come tax time. What you want is the real McCoy: someone who does this full-time and who bears the credential of C.F.P., or Certified Financial Planner. Most important of all, you want someone who will be objective.

Fee-only versus commission

For the sake of objectivity alone, you should look for a fee-only planner. Some planners derive their income from commissions made on the financial products they sell to customers. (This is why so many insurance agents and stockbrokers lay claim to be financial planners as well.) Fee-only planners don't. Rather, they charge a fee up front. (The fee should be determined by the hour.)

I'd suggest you avoid planners who work on straight commission or who charge you a percentage of the value of your portfolio. Someone working on straight commission cannot be unbiased. And a professional should provide the same level of service for someone with $5,000 as she or he would for someone with $5 million.

I think it's okay to consider planners who charge an hourly fee, but who also take some commissions, since they often do so to keep their hourly rates affordable. Unfortunately, many strictly fee-only planners charge a great deal of money and will only work with people who have very large investment portfolios. Until fee-only planners become the norm rather than the exception, you'll probably have to compromise.

Finding candidates and interviewing them

Finding the right planner should not be a matter of opening the phone book and chanting, "Eeny-meeny-miny-mo." You're looking for someone to help you invest your money! Don't you want the best?

Assuming your answer is yes, start by asking friends and relatives (particularly those who seem to be doing okay financially) if they can recommend someone. Another good way to get referrals is to ask the other professionals you deal with—attorneys, accountants—who they go to. You can also call the Institute of Certified Financial Planners (1-800-282-7526) and ask for a list of C.F.P.s in your area.

Questions to ask

Once you've got a few names, it's time to start interviewing potential planners. Anyone who won't see you in person, or who resists answering questions, should be crossed off your list immediately. Cooperative souls should be willing to tell you the following:

• How long they've been a planner, and how long they've been with this particular firm;
• What their firm's area of expertise is, and how long the firm has been around;
• Whether they work full- or part-time;
• Their educational background, including what advanced degrees they've earned;
• Whether they're an accredited member of a professional association (allowing use of the title certified financial planner, or the initials C.F.P.);
• The number of clients they have;
• How they continue to keep abreast of changes in the field;
• The average size of the portfolios they manage;
• What other services, if any, they provide;
• Whether they have any special investment strategies;
• Whether they're registered with the SEC;
• How they're compensated;
• What their best investment decision of the past few years has been;

• What their biggest investment blunder of the past few years has been.

Ask the planner to give you the names of three references whose circumstances are like your own. Again, if he won't, thank him for his time and cross him off your list. If you do get references, don't be shy about calling and asking the planner's clients if they've been pleased with the investments the planner has helped them make.

Questions to answer

One sign of a good planner is when, after answering your questions, the person puts a few to you. Before you arrange a meeting, be prepared for the planner to ask you the following:

• What are your assets and liabilities?
• What are your monthly expenses?
• What is your income and how secure is your job?
• What are your financial goals?
• What benefits does your employer offer?
• Are you married, and do you have children?
• What insurance coverage do you have, including life, health, property, and disability?
• Do you expect to inherit money at some point in the near or distant future?
• What is your philosophy of money?
• Is it important to you to do some money management on your own?
• How much risk are you willing to assume?

You're still in charge

Listen to your gut when it comes to choosing a financial planner. If someone strikes you as too smooth or slick, she probably is. If someone strikes you as not knowledgeable enough, he probably isn't. While you're not looking for someone to be your best buddy, you do need to choose someone you feel comfortable with, whom you can trust, and who'll do the best job for you.

You also need to look at this relationship as a partnership. The role of the planner is not to tell you what investment choices to make; nor should you let him assume that degree of control. Rather, he will make suggestions—suggestions which you can either approve or disapprove. But in order to do that, you need to be informed. That means, among other things, knowing how to read a mutual fund prospectus, so that when your planner comes to you and says, "I think you should look into investing in this fund," you can make an intelligent decision, not stick your head in the sand and say "Do whatever you think is best." I've said it before, and I'll say it again: It's your money. Take responsibility for it.

READING A MUTUAL FUND PROSPECTUS

The first time you're handed a mutual fund prospectus, your first inclination may be to hurl it across the room howling, "Boring, boring, boring!" or "You expect me to understand this?!" But, really, it's not that difficult. What you need to do is focus on a few key things, outlined below. Any questions you might have should be able to be answered by your financial planner; or you can call the fund's customer service number.

Costs

Most mutual fund prospectuses feature a table that gives readers a complete breakdown of costs and fees. Somewhere in the front of the prospectus there should also be a listing of what the annual operating costs are.

Investment objective

Most prospectuses list a primary objective, such as capital appreciation (otherwise known as growth); many will list a secondary objective as well, such as dividend income. When selecting a fund, make sure the fund's objectives match your own.

There's no point investing in an income fund if your goal is to make your money grow.

Investment techniques

This information is extremely important. If you're looking at a fund that's authorized to use risky or unusual investment strategies, you need to know that (and luckily, the prospectus will describe them). Any prospectus that mentions the word "derivative" when it comes to investment techniques is not one you want to invest in. Similarly, be wary of those funds that sell stocks short, or borrow money as a way of increasing their returns.

Management policies

This information is crucial as well, as it's really a listing of the securities (stocks and bonds) the fund means to purchase. Many list minimum and/or maximum percentage limitations for different types of investments. For example, the prospectus might read, "Fund manager is required to invest at least 60 percent of the fund's assets in foreign securities," or something along those lines.

Past performance

Past performance should be outlined in a table that shows performance figures from the fund for the past one, five, and ten years. (If the fund is less than a decade old, you'll see figures dating back to the fund's inception.)

In addition, the prospectus should give you a means against which you can measure the fund's performance, such as Standard & Poor's 500 Index. It should also show how the fund has performed in comparison with other mutual funds with the same investment objective.

Holdings

Some prospectuses list the fund's ten largest investments, while others list them all. If yours lists only ten and you feel you're not getting the whole picture, you can request a copy of the fund's most recent annual report. Also obtainable is what's known as the Statement of Additional Information, which many call Part B of the prospectus. Part B will list all the fund's investments.

Risk

Pretty self-explanatory, this part of the prospectus tells you the risks involved in the fund's investments. For example, funds investing overseas might be subject to currency risk. It is crucial that you read this section thoroughly and understand completely the risks involved.

Turnover

A listing of the annual turnover rate for investments should be included. Look for a fund with a low turnover.

Services

Some people want their funds to provide services like automatic payroll deduction or electronic exchange of funds within the same mutual fund family. These will be listed in the prospectus.

Manager

There will be a listing of the names, qualifications, tenure, and track record of your fund's manager or management team. Look for management continuity.

Minimum

The prospectus will state the minimum amount of money needed to open an account. (Note: Some funds will waive the minimum if you set up an automatic investment plan wherein you put in money into the account monthly.)

PICKING MUTUAL FUNDS

No doubt about it: Knowledge is power, and being able to read a mutual fund prospectus helps put you in the driver's seat (or at least the codriver's seat, next to your financial planner) when it comes to planning your investment strategy. But you need to be able to make sense of the information you've read to choose wisely (especially when you consider there are over 5,300 mutual funds available to choose from). As you go through a fund's prospectus, make sure the fund in question offers you:

• Above-average performance and below-average risk as determined by any unbiased rating, such as those in *Morningstar, Money, Worth,* etc.
• Consistency. Erratically performing funds should be avoided at all costs.
• A mix of styles. You don't want to own only one type of stock. Rather, you want to own a variety.
• Minimal expenses.
• Compatibility with your investment objective. Make sure the composition of the fund's investment portfolio is in keeping with the types of assets you want to hold.

Again, if you have any questions at all as to whether the fund adequately meets these criteria, talk to your official planner, or contact the mutual fund company for more information.

You're now at yet another crucial point in the process of turning your retirement dreams into reality. You know the different tools and techniques available to you. You can read a mutual fund prospectus, and hopefully now realize the importance of seeking out a financial planner to help you put flesh on the bones of your investment strategy. But before you can put your plan into action, you need to come up with the money to invest.

Unless you just happen to have a pile of money sitting around, or have just had a visit from Ed MacMahon or the Prize Patrol, you probably need to come up with the money. While far from easy or painless, raising money to invest is actually quite simple. Barring a sudden windfall, there are just three ways of doing that: you can cut your expenses, boost your income, or do both. Not coincidentally, cutting expenses is the subject of the next chapter.

15

CUTTING EXPENSES

Let me reiterate. Unless you've just received a gigantic inheritance or have savings already set aside, there are only three ways to come up with the money to invest for retirement: by cutting your expenses, increasing your stream of income, or both. This chapter is going to tell you how to cut expenses, a task that many people view as next to impossible. I'll let you in on a big secret: It isn't.

LIVING BENEATH YOUR MEANS

All it takes is the willingness to live beneath your means. Don't panic: I'm not going to tell you to sell your car or live off peanut-butter-and-jelly sandwiches for the next twenty years. What I am going to advise is that you take a long, hard look at your expenses, both fixed and variable; then I'm going to suggest some ways to cut them, thereby generating some money you can put toward your retirement dream.

Break down your expenses—in detail

Remember that back in Chapter 5 I asked to summarize your current living expenses in order to help you project what your expenses are likely to be in retirement? Well, it's time to go back over that two-part list of current expenses again, this time being as detailed as you can be about where your money goes.

For example, under the broad heading of "Entertainment," break the list down into such specific categories as "Books and CDs," "Cable TV fees," "Dining out," "Dues and memberships," "Movies, videos, plays, concerts, and sporting events," "Subscriptions," "Take-out," and "Vacations." Yes, this is more time-consuming than the thumbnail sketch of your finances you provided earlier, but it's in these details that you're going to find the resources you need to achieve your retirement dreams.

Focus first on fixed expenses

Once you've gone over the list with a fine-tooth comb and broken down all your expenses as minutely as possible, take a look at the "fixed" expenses, namely your rent or mortgage, your insurance payments, and your debt-related expenses, such as credit card bills. You probably assume that because they're called "fixed," you're powerless to change your monthly payments. You're wrong.

Reducing your mortgage payment

Check out the interest rates on home loans right now: they're pretty low. For that reason, it might make sense for you to refinance your mortgage, for lower monthly payments. The money you save can then be invested for retirement.

The trick is finding a bank or lending institution that's willing to absorb the fees involved so refinancing costs you nothing out-of-pocket. You might also want to consider switching to a fixed-rate mortgage if you've currently got a variable rate, or going for a thirty-year mortgage if you've got one that's for fifteen years. While it does mean it'll take you longer to pay the mortgage off, the money you'll be saving monthly can be put toward your retirement.

Reducing health insurance premiums

Many people are afraid of tinkering around with their health insurance, convinced that should an emergency arise, they won't be covered. The trick here is to figure out what you can cover yourself by choosing the highest deductible possible, and letting the insurance company take care of the rest. The higher your deductible, the lower your premium. The lower your premium, the more money you'll have for your retirement fund.

You might also see if there are ways of reconfiguring your medical coverage. With straight *major medical,* you select the doctor you're going to see and, in most cases, after meeting a deductible you're reimbursed completely for the money you lay out. But a smarter thing to do might be opting for *coinsurance,* under which you pay a certain amount (often 20 percent) in addition to meeting your deductible. After you reach a certain level of spending your coverage becomes total, protecting you from catastrophic bills. Coinsurance will usually lower your monthly premium more than enough to offset the cost of paying 20 percent of medical costs.

Other options worth exploring are *health maintenance organizations* (HMOs) and *health insurance plans* (HIPs). These plans require you to use participating doctors. Your insurance costs will be lowered, but you won't have complete control over who's watching out for your health. A new, and in my opinion much better, version of this has emerged—the *preferred provider organization* (PPO), where the insurance company covers some of the cost if you choose to see your own doctor, but will cover more if you use one of theirs.

I know what you're thinking. You hate to give up any control over your medical care. That's understandable. However, look at it this way: Give up some control over choosing your doctor now and in return you'll have enough money to gripe about it to your friends while you're all sitting around the pool in Tahiti Gardens.

Reducing your life insurance bill

Back in Chapter 11 we talked about the different types of life insurance available. As you may have sensed, I'm not too crazy about insurance as an investment, since I think you could do better elsewhere. Well, if I didn't convince you then, let me offer another argument now. If you want to save some money, investigate switching to term insurance from whole life or universal.

Similarly, make sure you're not overinsured. All you need to do is make sure you have enough insurance to cover funeral costs, pay for your kids' education if they're not yet out of college, and replace your income for two to three years, by which time, hopefully, your spouse will be there generating a sufficient income on his or her own, or will have made the required lifestyle adjustments.

Reducing disability insurance costs

Before I get into ways to save money on your disability coverage, let me impress upon you the importance of actually having disability coverage. Most people make the mistake of buying large life insurance policies and forgetting about disability coverage. That's a huge mistake, since most of us have a four times greater chance of becoming disabled between the ages of 35 and 65 than we do of going to the big coffee bar in the sky. If you don't have disability insurance, get some, even if it means postponing your retirement savings plan.

Okay, now let's look at some ways to save on your disability premiums. Since any benefits you receive from policies for which you pay the premium are tax-free, you really only need to buy enough to replace your take-home pay.

Second, bear in mind that if you become disabled, chances are your lifestyle is going to change and your expenses will be lower—no more commutation, lunches with clients, purchasing of work clothes—thus decreasing the necessary benefit even more.

Third, try to increase the duration of time between when you become disabled and when your benefits actually kick in. (Why? Because it's the equivalent of boosting your deductible.) For example, if you've got six months' worth of expenses put aside in a money market fund, theoretically you don't need your benefit payments to start for six months.

Reducing homeowners' insurance premiums

Go for the highest deductible you can. Yeah, you're thinking, but what if my kid's playing baseball in the yard and breaks a window, or there's a big storm and five shingles fly off the house? My answer is: So? Don't you have enough money to cover a lousy broken window or a few new shingles?

Homeowners' insurance isn't meant to cover the everyday wear and tear a house and its contents may take. It's meant to help you rebuild your home should it burn to the ground. Make sure your coverage is for the house only (also called "the existing structure"), not the surrounding property. In addition, make sure you're carrying insurance on only those items you'd have to replace were they lost or damaged. But what about my priceless collection of Tom Jones records? you're wondering. The key word here is "priceless." Since items like these are precious and simply can't be replaced, there's little point in paying for insurance coverage to replace them, wouldn't you agree?

Reducing your auto insurance bill

Many states require drivers to pay for a certain minimum amount of coverage, but if your insurance company is like most, you're paying a lot more than you have to. Find out what your state's minimum requirement is, and cut back as close as you can to that amount.

If your car is over three years old, ditch your collision coverage.

Similarly, if you have college-age kids, remove them from your policy (since, theoretically, they aren't regular drivers anymore).

If your policy covers goods stolen from the car, make sure they aren't also being covered in your homeowners' policy. You don't need to pay for the same coverage twice.

Similarly, if you belong to an auto club you don't need your auto insurance policy to cover towing. If it does, drop it. No need to pay twice for that either.

Reducing credit card debt and payment

No one likes having high-interest, nondeductible debt, yet few people realize that's exactly what they're doing when they use credit cards. To reduce credit card debt, start paying cash whenever you can. (More on this in a bit.)

If possible, pay off the balance on your credit cards and then cut them up and throw them away (except for one, which you can keep in case of emergency). If you've incurred a great deal of debt on multiple cards, look into obtaining a debt consolidation loan to help pay off the total while also making payments at a lower interest rate.

Speaking of interest rates, do you know what rate you're paying on your cards? Find out, then see if you can get a lower rate through some other institution.

Start keeping track of your cash

When it comes to cutting discretionary expenses, you first need to know where all your money is going—and I mean all. Most people can't account for all the money they spend over the course of each month. The reason? Credit cards and cash machines.

Think about how easy it is to whip out that piece of plastic to pay for something, or how convenient it is to go to a cash machine, press a few buttons, and, seconds later, be able to fill your wallet with crisp, clean dollar bills. While the amounts of money involved in these individual transactions might be small, over time they add up—without your being aware of it.

One of the best ways of cutting your discretionary expenses is to get your spending under control, and one of the best ways to do that is to wave bye-bye to credit cards and cash machines. That's right: Take your credit card and your cash card out of your wallet, and start carrying your checkbook around instead. Want to buy something? Write a check. The store won't accept a personal check? Schlep over to the bank and write out a check to "cash" for the exact amount you need.

The reasons for doing this are more psychological than anything else. Writing out a check takes time, effort, and, hopefully, genuine consideration. Every time you write a check, you've got to look at your checkbook ledger and subtract from your balance. In the best of all possible worlds, this should prompt you to think about what you're buying and whether you really, truly need it. Similarly, as you do the math required and watch your net worth decrease with every check you write, you'll inevitably find yourself comparing expenses. You'll find it educational, I'm sure.

CUTTING PERSONAL EXPENSES

Give yourself a few months to track your spending habits. Once you can account for where the money goes (down to the last dollar, if not penny), it's time to ask yourself the question many consider to be the most painful: Where can I cut back? Keep in mind that these cuts do not have to be monumental in size. More likely, you can make small cuts in both your fixed and variable personal expenses—cuts that will help boost your net worth if you turn around and take that money and invest it properly.

Don't believe a little bit can help? Well, if your late grandmother had saved $1 in 1925 and invested it for you in the stock of a good small company, it would have grown to more than $3,700 by her passing in 1995. Even if she was a lot more conservative and had invested that single greenback in a government bond, it would have been worth about $34 when she left it today. Change that $1 to $10, or $100 or $1,000, and look at the numbers again. Still think a little bit won't mean anything?

I didn't think so. That's why I've taken the liberty of offering some ways to start saving a little money in a lot of different areas.

Saving on entertainment, socializing, and dining out

• Brown-bag your lunch rather than hitting a restaurant or deli.

• Reduce the number of times you eat out per week.

• Reduce the number of times you purchase take-out per week.

• Rent movies rather than go to the theater. If you do go, see a matinee—it's cheaper (and less crowded).

• Throw potluck dinners rather than dinner parties.

• Meet friends for coffee and dessert rather than a full meal out.

• Bake your own cakes and cookies.

• Cook extra portions on the weekend that you can freeze or use as leftovers.

• Send your friends e-mail rather than making long-distance phone calls.

• Stop screening incoming calls. This ensures the caller is footing the bill, not you.

• Go vegetarian on 60 percent of the meals you cook. Meat costs.

• Buy wine instead of hard liquor, or beer instead of wine, and invest in a home water filtration system instead of shelling out constantly for the bottled variety.

• Take advantage of cheap and free entertainment, like free museum days, picnics, and concerts in the park.

Saving on food shopping

• Never shop without a list, and stick to that list when you hit the store.

• Clip coupons and compare unit prices.

• When you can, buy in bulk, or go generic.
• Be aware that produce prices are affected by the seasons.
• Investigate farmers' markets—sometimes they offer better quality for less money.
• Try store, local, and regional brands. They're often of equal quality at a lower cost since their producers don't pay for national ad campaigns.

Saving on health and medical expenses

• Don't renew your annual health club membership. Instead, invest in a one-time purchase like a cross-country ski machine, or put on your walking or running shoes and get out there and exercise on your own—it's free.
• If you must belong to a health club of some kind, look for the best price on a membership that offers the services you know you'll use.
• Ask your doctor to write out prescriptions for generic drugs wherever possible.
• Check around to see which pharmacy is the cheapest or if you can get prescriptions filled via mail order.
• Question your doctor when it comes to the cost of check-ups and procedures. If she or he charges more than what your insurance is willing to pay, find out why.
• Take care of yourself by eating properly and exercising regularly. In the long run, this will save you the most money of all—and help ensure that you'll live long enough to see retirement.

Saving on transportation expenses

• Make sure you really need two cars. Not only are you paying for the vehicles themselves, but there's maintenance, insurance, and registration and inspection fees.
• Pay attention to the regular maintenance of your car—oil changes, tune-ups—since that will help avoid larger bills.
• Buy or lease only as much car as you need. Cars are necessary evils, not status symbols.

- Walk, bike, or use public transportation whenever you can.
- Investigate carpooling.
- See if your boss will let you work for ten-hour days as opposed to five eight-hour days. Your commuting costs will be cut by at least 20 percent.

Saving on household and utilities expenses

- Wear a watch when you talk on the phone, or keep an egg timer nearby, so you can keep track of time.
- Make long-distance phone calls when rates are cheapest.
- Turn out the lights when you leave the room.
- Use low-wattage lightbulbs in your home except for those you read by.
- Turn your thermostat down to fifty when you leave the house and down to sixty when you go to bed at night.
- Don't use the dishwasher unless it's completely filled, and even then, use the energy-saving setting.
- Wash your clothes in cold, not warm, water. Line dry them if you can.
- Shower instead of taking a bath—it uses less water.
- Invest in low-flow shower and faucet heads, as well as a "coat" for your hot water heater.
- If you need to purchase an appliance, don't go top-of-the-line. When it comes to washers, dryers, etc., opt for the more economical large-capacity models, and use them less frequently.
- If you can, heat your home with gas rather than electricity or oil.
- Ever hear of planned obsolescence? Fight it. Maintain your TV, VCR, stereo, computer, and other appliances so they last longer.
- Do your own car repair, home repair, painting, and sewing.
- Barter with your neighbors. Maybe you could baby-sit one afternoon in exchange for having your lawn mowed and your hedges trimmed. The possibilities are endless.

Saving on vacations and travel costs
- Travel off-season.
- Purchase airline tickets well in advance of travel if you can.
- Fly midweek with a weekend stay. Those rates are the cheapest.
- If you travel a lot, join a frequent-flyer club.
- Avoid luxury hotels (unless someone else is paying for it, of course).
- If you're afraid of flying, get help or get over it. Rail, ship, and auto transportation are all much more expensive.
- Investigate taking the bus. Long-distance buses have improved a great deal over the past ten years, particularly those that service college towns and therefore have a regular clientele. The trip may be only a little bit longer than making the drive yourself. In addition, you can rest or work while on the trip.

Saving on gift expenses
- Make your own gifts. Believe me, people love this, especially if the gift is baked goods. (Nothin' says lovin' like somethin' from the oven, as the saying goes.)
- Establish a budget when it comes to buying presents, and stick to it.
- For big holidays like Hanukkah or Christmas, set up a gift pool where each member of the family is responsible for buying a present for one other member of the family. (This is especially helpful if you have a large family or if there are lots of little 'uns.)

Some other ways to save
- Cut back on magazine subscriptions. Only subscribe to those magazines or newspapers you read religiously from cover to cover. Otherwise buy individual issues on the newsstand.
- Get a library card and make regular visits to the library. In case you haven't noticed, libraries today stock not only the

latest bestsellers, but videos, CDs, and computer games, and often offer Internet access.

• Quit smoking and/or drinking. Not only are both expensive but they'll cost you in medical care down the road.

• Don't shop for "fun." Shop when you have something you definitely need to buy. If you want to get out of the house, take your spouse, child, or dog for a walk.

• Don't buy any more new clothing until every item currently in your closet is paid for.

• Frequent garage sales and secondhand shops. You wouldn't believe the bargains you can find, especially in affluent areas.

• Try to shop at discount centers and factory warehouses whenever you can. The ambience might not be great, but the savings can be.

• Double-check all computer-generated bills that come in. It's not uncommon to be overcharged.

• If a service charge is included in a bill when you're dining out, don't tip. If you are in a situation where tipping is customary, leave 15 percent for acceptable service, 20 percent for exceptional service, or 10 percent for crummy service.

• Adjust your withholding tax. It's possible that too much money is being withheld from your paycheck—money you could use. If there's a chance your income might drop this year, or if you got a tax refund last year or have a feeling that your deductible expenses might rise this year, investigate the possibility of decreasing the taxes withheld, and saving the added take-home pay.

CUTTING BUSINESS EXPENSES

Just as cutting personal expenses can help you come up with cash to invest for your retirement, so can trimming your business expenses, especially if you're a small business owner whose finances are directly tied to the business.

The process begins in the same way. First you need to take stock (no pun intended) of where every penny goes. Most small businesses have four main areas in which they incur expenses: labor, rent, insurance, and marketing. Let's take a look at each, and see where you might be able to trim some fat.

Labor

Unless you run a one-man or one-woman shop, labor is probably your largest expense. Take a careful look at your payroll. How many employees (full-time, part-time, and temporary) do you have? Have many of those employees have assistants? How many of those assistants have assistants?

Now comes the hard part.

Ask yourself: "Do the members of my staff (including me) really need these assistants, or were the assistants hired so that the person in charge could delegate tasks he or she didn't want to do?" Ask yourself:

• Can I replace a full-timer with a part-timer without impacting the quality of what I offer my clients or customers?
• Can I replace a part-timer with a temp without impacting the quality of what I offer my clients or customers?
• Can I do without a temp without reducing the quality of what I offer my clients or customers?

If you answer yes to any or all of these questions then you're going to have to let some people go.

This is not a pain-free decision, nor should it be. No one wants to be the bad guy who fires someone and casts that person out into an economically uncertain world. But you can't let your emotions cloud your economic judgment.

If you do have to make a termination or terminations, it makes sense to look first at the low folks on the totem pole. The higher-ups have more to lose and should be willing to shoulder more of a burden. To assuage the guilt you'll no doubt feel, make sure you offer the person a decent severance package. Just make sure remaining staffers are aware that these worker bees are not going to be replaced; rather, you'll be expecting everyone to pitch in and pick up the slack.

Another way to cut expenses when it comes to labor is to consider a moratorium on hiring, even if your company is expanding. Additional work can always be farmed out to freelancers, temps, or part-timers, and that will save you money since you won't have to pay for any benefits.

Also consider whether you can really afford to give bonuses and raises, and if so, how much. You might also think of doing away with Christmas gifts. Will you be perceived as a Scrooge? It depends. If you implement the changes and inform staff about them by circulating a memo, then yes, you will.

What you need to do is put a human face on these layoffs and cutbacks, by calling a meeting and explaining that all the changes are economic, not personal. Explain that you won't be hiring new staff and that you yourself will be picking up some of the slack and you expect the same from them, too. Most crucial of all, tell your staff that your goal is actually to save jobs by cutting costs. Those who have escaped the ax will be grateful, as well as appreciative of your honesty.

Rent

High rents can eat up a sizable portion of your profit. Luckily, prices in commercial real estate are falling, which gives you some leverage with your landlord when it comes to renegotiating.

Approach him and say that your bank has been pressuring you to lower costs as a condition to renegotiating your next long-term loan. Offer to strike a bargain: if he will reduce your rent for the next few years, you promise to stay on as tenant for an additional five. If the landlord balks, see if you can at least get him to assume the costs of any improvements you might want to make.

Another way to cut expenses when it comes to rent is by consolidating locales. Let's say your business operations are spread out over three locations. Rentwise, it might be savvy to find one large space from which to operate rather than paying for rent on three.

If your business is small enough, consider working from home.

Insurance

Business coverage usually falls into two categories: property/casualty coverage and employee benefits. To cut down on property and casualty coverage, ask three or four reputable brokers to bid on your coverage. He who comes up with the best cost savings package for you, wins.

Cutting employee benefits is tricky, but if you absolutely have to, it can be done. The best way to cut the largest part of the coverage—health insurance—is to implement coverage that involves cost sharing and managed care. Cost sharing means taking a higher deductible and adding a coinsurance element (if you don't have one already) wherein employees cover more of the cost of their own care. Managed care involves putting in place certain regulations that can reduce costs, such as preadmission testing and getting a second opinion before surgery. HMOs also fall under the mantle of managed care, as do PPOs.

More and more companies are cutting health costs by encouraging employees to take care of themselves. You can have regular health assessments done twice a year at your office, or offer bonuses to those employees who quit smoking or lose weight. Such measures boost corporate morale in addition to being preventative: they show employees you really care about them.

Other insurance costs can be cut by finding out who in your employ could obtain coverage through a spouse's plan rather than yours. This doesn't mean denying the person coverage completely—for example, you could still offer him or her disability coverage. There are many variations in the types of coverage you can offer individual employees—and many of them could result in increased savings for you.

Marketing

Most businesses take their marketing dollars and spread them across a variety of media. While this advertising approach is far-reaching, it's also wasteful. Instead, concentrate your marketing dollars on where you know your customers are. This involves doing some informal market research. Obtain as much info as you can about your customers by talking to them, or by looking through warranty cards or guest books. Then compare the profile you come up with to the profile of a radio station's listener, a TV station's viewer, or a magazine's subscriber. Whichever profile matches best with yours is where your marketing money should be spent.

Do what you can to obtain free media publicity as well. If there's something unique or interesting about your business, see if you can't get a reporter from the local paper or radio or TV station to do a story on it. Such stories are usually much more effective than ads, which people know you pay for.

Saving in other areas

While labor, rent, insurance, and marketing are probably the areas that offer the most opportunities for cuts, they aren't the only ones. Below are some other strategies for reducing business expenses.

• Buy your business cards, forms, and stationery at a lower cost by utilizing a mail-order stationery company or local print shop, or by generating them yourself with your own equipment.
• Become more visible in your community. Potential customers are everywhere, which is one reason it makes sense to become active in the civic arena. It will also give you the opportunity to network with other small business owners.
• Buy office supplies at a discount.
• Produce ads in-house if possible, rather than farming them out to an agency.
• Buy office furniture used.
• Pay business expenses this year rather than waiting until

next year. The more expenses you can deduct, the smaller your tax bill will be.

• Cut back on entertaining customers.

• Call your professionals and ask them to bill you on an hourly basis with a budget, or to lower their retainers.

• Eliminate all unnecessary memberships in clubs and associations.

• Do your own bookkeeping. Doing the bookkeeping for a small business isn't really that difficult, especially if you invest in a computer software program to help you. In addition, there are companies that offer "one write" checkbook systems, which allow you to make accounting entries whenever you write out a check or make a deposit. If you absolutely must have someone else take care of the books, look into hiring a low-cost service to do it out-of-house.

• Hold staff parties in the office and at lunch rather than out at a restaurant for dinner.

• Bill on a regular basis. Too many business owners let collections get away from them. Don't be one of them; make sure you prepare—and send out—your bills on a regular basis.

• If you anticipate your business moving into a higher tax bracket next year, accumulate as much profit as you can this year by billing this year and speeding up the collection of receivables.

• Cut down on the number of magazine subscriptions that come to the office. There's nothing wrong with buying one copy of a magazine and then circulating it.

• Figure out which overnight delivery service is the cheapest and use it only sparingly. Ditto with the fax machine.

• Trade services for advertising. Just as I advocated bartering with your neighbors, so too can you barter in business, especially if you can hook up with an advertiser who might be willing to throw you some freebies in exchange for your providing some applicable goods and services.

• Ask the local utility service to conduct an energy audit

at your location and implement any cost-cutting suggestions they make.

• Negotiate lower interest rates on business loans, and make sure your business loans maximize tax benefits.

• Encourage free, word-of-mouth advertising whenever you can. Not only is it the cheapest form of advertising, it's also the form that works best.

• Take advantage of lower evening and weekend phone rates. Most entrepreneurs or small business owners work in the evenings as well as on the weekend. Why not make your calls or even send faxes when rates are cheapest?

• If you're considering selling all or part of your business, time the sale so the taxes you have to pay are minimal, or even postponed.

Cutting personal and business expenses doesn't need to be painful. Trim a little here, tighten the belt there, and before you know it, you've got spare money in your pocket. It doesn't even have to be a huge amount of money! Remember that $1 your grandparents could have invested: a small amount of cash invested wisely can go a long way.

Of course, cutting expenses isn't the only way to generate that money; you can also boost revenues. Read all about that by turning to the next chapter.

16

BOOSTING REVENUES

Okay, so you've gotten down to the business of cutting expenses. You've canceled your subscription to *Fly Fishing Monthly,* and your kids know there will be hell to pay if they leave lights on around the house. Now it's time to implement your other strategy for raising funds for retirement investing: increasing your stream of income.

In general, there are four ways you can do this: get a raise, moonlight, start a part-time business, or find a new, higher-paying job. Let's examine them individually.

ASKING FOR A RAISE

Of all the anxiety-producing scenarios that can occur in the workplace, number one on the list is asking for a raise. We fear being rejected, or worse, laughed at. We fear it will affect our job security. Yet it is precisely this fear that could keep you from getting the money you deserve. The first step in asking for a raise, then? Letting go of your fear.

I know this is easier said than done, but think about it: What your employer pays you is simply a reflection of what he or she thinks your services are worth. Thus, it's subjective. Furthermore, your salary isn't synonymous with your worth as a human being. Until you realize that, you're going to find it difficult to approach the process of getting a raise in a rational way.

It might help to contemplate this: Your employer is just as afraid of talking to you about a raise as you are of asking for one. He or she is going to be sitting behind that big, overpriced mahogany desk, wondering: Is this employee gonna walk if I don't give her an adequate raise? Do we as a company, in fact, pay fairly? Knowing that your boss is anxious as well can be a useful negotiating tool for you, as you'll soon discover.

Perhaps you've been told that your company has a "system" when it comes to pay raises, so asking for a raise is futile. Don't believe it. This is usually a smoke screen used by upper management to keep the worker ants in their place. But even if there is a system, who says you can't buck it? Especially if your job description has changed, or you're contributing a helluva lot more to the company than you're being paid.

Since it's obvious you're going to have to take matters into your own hands:

Start by doing research on your company

Are there, in fact, guidelines for raises? What are these guidelines based on? How strictly are they enforced? Can they be circumvented if circumstances warrant it? If you can, find out what the guy in the next cubicle, doing the same job as you, is making. Most crucial is seeing if you can find out who in the company has the real power to grant your raise request.

If you kept the research you originally gathered on your company from when you were job-hunting, look at it, then update it. Note whether the company's health has improved since you've been aboard.

Figure out your value on the current job market

This isn't as hard as it sounds: all you need do is check with competing companies, trade associations, the Bureau of Labor

Statistics, employment agencies, headhunters, the want ads, or even trade magazine surveys. Any of these sources should be able to give you a fair estimate of what your salary should be. If you want, you can use this process as a springboard to start searching for a new job, one where you'll be paid your value.

Honestly assess your job performance

Are you a team player, if that's what is required? Has your job profile changed since you started? Can your contribution to the company be documented? If you can, make a list of everything you've done, implemented, supervised, created, and so on. Not only will it boost your self-esteem, but it will provide you with concrete evidence you can present to a supervisor who might be unaware of the details of your job performance. You can also use it as an outline when dealing with your boss.

Time the discussion of your raise

There are good times and bad times to ask for a raise. Mondays and Fridays are out. If you can, try to schedule the meeting for Tuesday, Wednesday, or Thursday, either in the late afternoon or the early morning. Some other things to think about when it comes to timing:

• If, during your last salary negotiation, you and your boss agreed to a review date, stick to it.

• If no review date was established at your last negotiation, wait at least one year between requests for raises. The exceptions? If your previous increase was an interim measure, or if your job responsibilities have changed dramatically. If you've got a gut feeling that waiting might actually help, not hurt, your chances for success, you may want to wait longer.

• You want to make sure to ask for a raise at the start of a new selling season, or before annual budgets are drawn up.

• There are instances where waiting might actually hurt your negotiating power, resulting in your being offered a token increase. Better to grab the bull by the horns and take control.

*   *   *

Be aware that it's a waste of your time, as well as your boss's, to walk into a meeting to negotiate a raise without having an actual dollar figure in your head. Without it, the focus of the discussion will shift to whether or not you deserve the raise—which is not the issue you want to debate. Offer a figure and it becomes the center of the discussion.

The figure you propose at the meeting should be based on your research as well as an honest appraisal of your needs. An inflated figure will only result in your not being taken seriously, so avoid the temptation to put an astronomical number on the table.

Observe raise-negotiation etiquette

One of the reasons most of us would rather endure a PBS pledge drive than ask for a raise is that we have no idea how to conduct ourselves at such a meeting, and thus feel great trepidation. Obviously you don't want to storm in and say, "Pay me what I'm worth or I'm outta here, Bucko." Rather, the first words out of your mouth should be, "I love my job, but I have a problem and I need your help with it." While stating your case—and stressing that the figure you've arrived at is reasonable and based on research geared to your market value—make sure you:

- Project warmth without appearing to be too friendly.
- Maintain direct eye contact.
- Refer to the company, not your boss, as your employer.
- Listen more than you speak. If gaps in the conversation arise, don't scramble to fill them. Leave that to your boss.
- End the meeting if your boss seems distracted or uninterested.
- Blow your own horn. Now is not the time for humility.
- Don't waffle. Show some backbone.
- Absorb or deflect expressions of anger or resentment.
- Act as you would in any other business meeting.

• Leave the chip off your shoulder. If you don't, not only will you walk out without a raise, you might walk out without a job.

• Don't make demands or threaten.

• Don't project guilt. Remember, you deserve this.

• Don't nod when your employer speaks. He or she might take it as a concession to terms you have no intention of agreeing to.

• Don't say "sir"—you're not this person's butler or chauffeur, much as he might like you to be. Instead, use "Mr." before his name—or, for a woman, "Ms." or "Mrs."

Rebut employer responses

All your energies must be focused on one specific point: that what you're currently being paid no longer matches your contributions, either because your job description has changed or because you've accomplished so much on the job.

Be prepared for your boss to come up with a multitude of reasons why you can't have this raise. Your best defenses? A calm, calculated refutation. Below, some excuses you're likely to hear, as well as how you should respond:

"You haven't been here long enough to merit a raise."

Your response: "I don't think you can fairly measure my value to the company by the length of time I've worked here. Let's look at what I've accomplished since I began working here."

"We have a policy of . . ." or "How can I pay you more than I pay Hedges?"

Your response: "Let me make sure I understand. You're saying that no matter how hard I work or how successful I am here, I won't be rewarded for it? I always thought that excellence was rewarded here."

"We just don't have the money right now to give you a raise."

Your response: "I understand. If the money's not there, the money's not there. But maybe we can agree to an increase that would take effect in six months. In the meantime, there are some nonfinancial areas I need to speak with you about. For example, I'd like three more personal days . . ." (or whatever other nonfinancial compensation you'd be willing to take instead).

There are two ways your boss can go from there. Either he'll say he can't guarantee the money but he'll okay whatever nonfinancial compensation you're looking to secure, or he'll dig in his heels and claim both requests are contrary to company policy. In either case, your response should be, "I understand. But I need to leave here with a definite date for our next discussion. How about five months from today? Also, I'd appreciate it if you could double-check about those personal days."

End the meeting, and start looking for another job.

"I find it hard to believe you're being underpaid. Let me see your numbers. These figures come from companies that are bigger than ours. If you check your numbers again, you'll see we pay competitive wages."

Your response: "I don't want what I'm not entitled to. If you think my research is incomplete, I'd be glad to do more and come back to you with it in a couple of weeks. What companies do you consider comparable to ours?"

While it's possible that your boss will offer you other sources to look at, chances are your throwing the ball back in his court will result in his saying, "I'd have to think about it. But I'm sure you're not being underpaid."

In either case, tell him you will look into the issue further and come back to him with more results. In the meantime, you want to nail down a time for that meeting.

Be Prepared for Compromises

Don't be surprised if your employer tries to take control of the situation by making you a compromise offer. ("I won't give you a raise, but from now on, you don't have to clean the coffee machine anymore. How 'bout that?")

While your natural inclination might be to say, "Screw you, pal," and walk, the better choice would be asking for another meeting a week hence, then using the interim time to think about it. You'll be able to consider the offer, regain control of the situation, and reformulate your request, adding any arguments you might have forgotten or overlooked. The simple truth is, the longer you keep the raise issue under his nose, the better your chances of getting one will be.

Of course, there is the possibility that your request will be met with a resounding no, and that your employer will refuse to discuss the issue any further. If that's the case, thank Mussolini for his time and start looking for another job.

What's more likely to happen is that you'll be offered a token increase. Will you feel insulted? Probably. But rather than stew over it, try to get a commitment to renegotiate the issue in the near future. When the next meeting rolls around, mount your appeal. Unless your boss is a totally tightfisted automaton, he or she will have a hard time turning you down twice. Bolster your argument with new facts you've dug up, and ask for a reinterpretation in light of this new evidence.

If you're rejected again, it's time to ask yourself some hard questions. Do you really want to stay at a company that undervalues your contribution and doesn't pay you your worth? Hopefully, your answer will be no. In that case, it's time to look for another job—which we'll get to in a few pages.

The optimal position to be in when asking for a raise is to have another job offer. If that's your situation, set up the meeting and say, "I have to tell you that I've been approached by another firm, which has offered me a sizable salary increase.

While I would much rather stay on here, I really have to think about my own/my family's security.''

Either your boss will match or exceed the other company's offer, in which case you've got your raise, or he'll say, "I wish you all the best in your new job. Have your desk cleared out by Friday," in which case you'll also have gotten a raise— once you call the other company to tell them you're accepting their offer. Either way, you win.

MOONLIGHTING

Moonlighting is the time-honored tradition of holding down a second job. The reasons for doing so almost always come down to the same: to make more money. In your case, however, you wouldn't be moonlighting to make ends meet. Rather, you'd be working that second job as a way to generate spare cash to invest for your retirement.

Before you even consider holding down a second job, you need to sit down and talk to your partner about it. Chances are that he or she works as well, so you need to examine how your moonlighting could impact the family's schedule. For example, if you're the one responsible for doing the laundry or the food shopping, where do you think you'll find the time to reschedule that activity? Will your getting a second job mean you'll have to pay for child care? (If so, it might not be worth it, as the money you'll be earning could be eaten up in paying a baby-sitter or day care center.)

Most important of all, how will working a second job impact the time you get to spend with your children? You can always make more money, but you can't repeat the day your daughter hits her first home run in Little League. If being an integral part of your children's lives is important to you—and moon-lighting will interfere with it—bypass this option entirely and do whatever you can to get a raise or a new job, and/or cut expenses to the bone.

When looking for a second job, try to find something that's

in a different sector than the job you currently work. There are a couple of reasons for this. One, you don't want to risk having a conflict of interest on your hands; and two, you don't want your attention divided in any way. Your energy should always go toward your primary job.

For that reason alone, see if you can get something that offers weekend rather than evening hours. The reason? To avoid scheduling conflicts. What if your company schedules an after-hours meeting, or a late-day meeting simply runs overtime? What are you going to say—"Sorry, but I have to leave, I'm late for my job at Tooty's Clam Shack"? That's not going to go over too well.

In fact, if you do get a second job, you should probably keep it to yourself. There's no reason your boss needs to know you've got another gig on the side. Similarly, if the boss at your second job asks why you don't want full-time work, don't tell him you have a full-time job already. (No one, especially a business owner, likes to be told he's second on someone's priority list.) Instead, tell him that you've decided to go back to school for your doctorate, but in the meantime you need to bring in some cash.

One of the good things about moonlighting is that you don't have to worry about benefits or advancement—it's already being taken care of via your full-time job. As for taxes on the money you'll earn, working off-the-books is an illegal, albeit common wait, of maximizing your income. But whether your part-time boss cooks the books or not, see if you can arrange to have your paycheck deposited directly into your account. This will remove any temptation you might have to treat this added income as "mad money" and spend it frivolously.

The main drawbacks to moonlighting are your lack of control when it comes to salary and the hours you'll work, and being at the beck and call of yet another employer. No wonder so many folks interested in generating more income choose not to moonlight, but to start part-time businesses instead.

STARTING A PART-TIME BUSINESS

If accruing more money via a part-time job appeals to you but having to answer to yet another suit doesn't, starting your own part-time business might be the way to go. There are three types worth checking out: home-based consulting, itinerant selling, and mobile service. Below, a consideration of each.

Home-based consulting biz

In case you haven't noticed, we're in the middle of a workplace revolution. More and more people, tired of the drain on commuting as well as the lack of freedom and security that's part of working in an office, are electing to work from home instead, both full- and part-time. In fact, it's estimated that the total number of Americans working from home, at least part-time, numbered close to 45 million in 1994.

Most of these people were working out of their homes as consultants; that is, they provide services and professional advice to consumers or businesses. For example, someone who's comptroller of a small publishing company by day could, by night or on weekends, prepare taxes for people from her home.

To be a successful part-time, home-based consultant, you need to be an expert in your field as well as being a good problem solver. Apparently, lots of people are: according to *The Wall Street Journal*, income from home-based consulting businesses hovered around $10.5 million in 1995.

But before you let fantasies of turning the mud room into your own private office run away with you, you really need to think about whether this option is right for you. Most people who work out of their home—and are successful at it—are extremely disciplined.

Further, you need to pinpoint exactly what it is you'd be consulting on. Start by grabbing a piece of paper and a pen and jotting down all your skills as well as areas of expertise. Don't feel that any area is too arcane or silly. If you're an expert on the history of rock 'n' roll or the fighter planes of World War II, write it down. When you're done, list all the tasks you're able to perform, as well as those tasks you can train others to perform. Now go over your list again, pondering the following:

• Is there a market out there for this kind of skill and knowledge?
• If so, who would my clients be?
• What kinds of problems can I solve for individuals or businesses?

As is the case with any job, there are pros and there are cons, and part-time, home-based consulting is no exception. Below, some of the advantages:

You don't have to commute

This can be especially appealing if a good part of getting to and from your day job is spent in the car or riding mass transit.

When not meeting clients, you don't have to dress for work

While some observers believe you should "dress" for home-based work as a way of getting into a work mindset and reminding yourself that you are indeed a professional, I don't. I've met deadlines sitting in my robe and fuzzy slippers and have churned out copy in paint-spattered sweatpants. As long as you're comfortable and motivated, the work will get done.

You can set your own hours

Too pooped to work at night but rarin' to go at seven A.M. on Saturdays and Sundays? There are limits, but when you have your own business, you can make flextime a company policy and work those hours. It's one of the beauties of working at home. If you're someone who likes to set strict working hours, do so. It's up to you.

It's cheap to start

In most instances, start-up costs for part-time, home-based consulting businesses are minimal. You might have to invest in some computer equipment, but that's bound to be far less than the cost of renting office space.

It can be a tax advantage

Working from home, you'll be able to write off a portion of your expenses, including rent or mortgage, utilities, and telephone. If your business is one in which clients come to your home, you might even be able to write off a portion of house-cleaning services and lawn care.

Now for the disadvantages:

You can never escape from work

Unlike working in an office, from which you can physically and well as psychologically depart, working at home offers no respite. You can be sitting on the couch watching *Seinfeld* with the family when your business lines rings. Do you ignore it or get it? Either way, the call has interrupted you. If you're a workaholic, working at home can be extremely problematic, as you might be tempted to devote every free minute of your time to your job, to the chagrin of your family and the neglect of your other responsibilities.

Your "real life" can be a distraction

What will you do when a call to a client is interrupted by your teenager blasting Nine Inch Nails on his stereo? If you can't control or ignore distractions, a home-based biz might not be for you. Further, many people find it hard to resist the lure of leisure activities when they're the master of their own schedule.

You lack the space

Not every home has a spare room just ready and waiting to be converted into an office. More often than not, people find themselves clearing a corner of the bedroom or den and setting up their business there. It can work—but be prepared for major interruptions and distractions.

There's no place to meet clients

Meeting clients at home is not only inconvenient, in many instances it's unprofessional. What are you going to do, usher them downstairs to your basement lair and ask them take a seat next to the oil burner? Instead, ask a local restaurant owner if she wouldn't mind your lingering over a meal a few times a week. She'll appreciate the business, and you'll have yourself a pleasant, professional atmosphere in which to meet.

The phone can drive you batty

Believe me, this is a biggie. While a ringing phone is a sign your business is doing well, it can also drive your family screaming from the house, especially if you don't have a second phone line for business. But even if you do, turn your answering machine on after "business hours." It's the only way to ensure some semblance of a life.

It can be a struggle to keep up with developments in your field

If you're billing yourself as an expert, you'd better be up on the latest news in your field. This means subscribing to relevant magazines, newspapers, and newsletters—and finding the time to read them. It also means maintaining contact with others in your field by attending conferences, seminars, and other information-gathering venues. Be aware that while some clients will make their way to you of their own volition, the majority will have to be cultivated, and then maintained. That means getting your butt out there and selling your services.

TIME FOR A REALITY CHECK

If you're like most people, the idea of a part-time, home-based consulting business probably sounds great to you. But in reality, not everyone is cut out for it. In order to be successful at this kind of business, you need to be the kind of person who can deliver on your claim to be an expert, and you also need to have what it takes to work from home.

Successful consultants:

• Are willing to do research, solve problems, and provide solutions;
• Know their area of expertise well enough that they're able to convince others that they can teach them what they need to know, or that they can maximize their profits/or streamline their businesses;
• Can go out there and create their own client base.

Successful home-based entrepreneurs:

• Are extremely disciplined and self-sufficient;
• Can handle working alone (in fact, most prefer it);
• Are confident about making decisions on their own;
• Are aggressive about pursuing and maintaining clients;
• Are undaunted by minor setbacks.

Additionally, if you're going to be doing your consulting part-time you must be able to keep your full-time job profile as high as, if not higher than, before, while simultaneously investing considerable effort into your part-time business. How is that possible? By working long hours and having a great deal of energy.

DIFFERENT KINDS OF CONSULTANTS

Let's say you've really thought it through, and you've decided to give part-time, home-based consulting a whirl. As mentioned earlier, all consultants are problem solvers. All help clients examine a problem, develop a plan to tackle it, then implement and fine-tune the plan so the problem is eradicated.

But before you hang a shingle outside your house or take

out a full-page ad in the local paper, you need to decide which kind of consultant you're going to be: a consumer consultant or a business consultant.

Consumer consultants help consumers make personal decisions. Hence, a consumer consultant can be anything from a financial planner to a tarot card reader. Consumer consultants need not offer services related to the areas in which they work full-time. Instead, they have the option of consulting in any areas that interest them. The trick is making yourself stand out from the pack and convincing potential clients they need you and not the guy up the street who's doing the same thing.

Business consultants offer clients the years of experience and expertise they have in specific areas, whether the area is training and education or management. Businesses use consultants to advise them in myriad areas. To land a gig as a business consultant, you need to show potential clients specific skills and talents you have that will enhance their business.

To figure out whether your strengths lie in business or personal consulting, answer the following questions as honestly as you can.

- What do I enjoy doing for others?
- What are my hobbies and passions?
- Do I prefer working indirectly or directly with others?
- What business experience do I have?
- What training have I had in different areas?
- What are my specific skills?
- What would I consider my accomplishments to be?
- What skills and knowledge will I need to bring to the area of consulting I'm interested in?
- Who would my competition be in this region?
- If competition is fierce, would I be willing to consult outside this immediate area, either through traveling or electronically?

GETTING STARTED

So it's a go? You definitely want to consult in some way, shape, or form? Before you do anything, you need to figure out who your ideal client is—the person or business that will be clamoring for your services.

Once you've got a handle on that, you need to determine if there are enough people or businesses out there to support your consulting. The process differs depending upon whether you want to be a personal or business consultant.

Guidelines for the potential business consultant

The narrower and more defined your target market, the better your chances of success. Imagine your future clients, coming up with an image of which businesses might need your services, as well as an image of the people who run those businesses. Let's say you have the skill, experience, and inclination to become a consultant on advertising and marketing. It follows, then, that you might look at local businesses that don't seem to be reaching the potential customer base they could. Find out who owns these businesses.

Before approaching these owners with a plan, you'll need to "credentialize" yourself as an expert in advertising and marketing. This can be done by giving seminars or talks, or publishing related articles and books. It's also necessary to network until you drop, in the hopes that you become known in your field within the business community.

Once you've come up with a list of which businesses you think could use your expertise, you need to figure out how large your potential customer base is. Start by looking at the community you live in. Is it up-and-coming? Are there businesses of different sizes here that could use your help? Or could you benefit from building a client base via the Internet?

Next, figure out who owns these businesses, and go after them. This means getting involved in your community, as well as attending functions at the chamber of commerce and the local businesspersons' association.

If there's a sufficient base to support your proposed endeavor, get in touch with other consultants, but not those who are doing the exact same thing you plan on doing (for obvious reasons, they won't be very forthcoming with information). Find out how the consultants got started, where they advertise their services, how their business strategies have changed. Ask them what they'd change if they had it to do all over again, as well as what their greatest triumphs and failures have been. Ask them to describe their clients to you in as much detail as possible.

Once you've picked the brains of some pros and have a potential customer base, test your idea by running it by potential clients. Ask any business executives you know whether they need the service you're offering. Cull names from chamber of commerce listings, new business openings listed in the paper, or the yellow pages, and then call. Find out if it's a service they'd be interested in and, if so, how much they'd be willing to pay.

Another avenue worth exploring is contacting an independent observer via your local SBA (Small Business Administration) office, as I suggested in Chapter 1. The SBA sponsors a mentor program called SCORE, or Service Corps of Retired Executives, wherein retired businesspeople offer their insights to people launching their own businesses. Not only will you get impartial advice from a seasoned professional, it won't cost you a cent.

Guidelines for the potential personal consultant

The process of starting a personal consulting business is essentially the same when it comes to locating your target customers and gleaning information from other consultants, with a few minor differences when it comes to figuring out who your client is and where to find her or him.

Those interested in starting a personal consulting business need to imagine their clients as vividly as possible. Are they men, women, or both? Where do they live, how much money do they earn, what are their hobbies? Where do they shop?

Once you've got an image of your customers in your mind,

check out places that might sell them services or products related to yours, and indulge in some people-watching. Get in touch with relevant trade groups for demographic information you can use to fine-tune your image of them. As I said earlier, the sharper your focus, the better your chances for success.

Like those interested in carving a niche for themselves as business consultants, personal consultants also need to run their plans by potential clients. In your case, it can be just about anyone: family, friends, neighbors. Don't be afraid of going door-to-door to solicit opinions, or of making cold calls on the phone. The worst that can happen is that you're hung up on or told to buzz off. So what? It's their loss.

No matter which area of consulting you're interested in, these pointers should help you get started. From there on in, though, the process gets quite complex, too complex to examine here. For that reason, I'd advise you to check out one of the following books for more details on how to get your own part-time, home-based consulting business off the ground:

• *How to Start a Home Business,* by Michael Antoniak (Avon Books, 1995).
• *How to Start a Retirement Business,* by Jacqueline Powers (Avon Books, 1996).
• *How to Start a Freelance Consulting Business,* by Jacqueline Powers (Avon Books, 1998).

Traveling sales business

For most business owners, their largest expense is the rent or mortgage they have to pay for the space they occupy. But if you're a traveling seller, you don't have to worry about this, since you have no fixed place of business. Instead, you go where there's a demand for your services, whether it's the parking lot at a sports event, a craft fair, or a busy city street corner. What are the advantages and disadvantages of such a business? Read on.

The advantages of this type of business are many. They include:

You provide customers with a product they want as efficiently and directly as possible

All of us these days are crunched for time. No one wants to dash into a crowded mall to buy flowers for the wife on the way home when he can grab a bouquet at the train station before catching the commuter express. Itinerant sellers appeal to buyers because they save them time and energy. In addition, they often sell items that can't be found in the average department store. The advantage to you as the owner of such a business? No overhead or storefront to maintain. You're peripatetic in the truest sense of the word—whither the demand is, you will follow.

You determine your own work schedule, whether it's seasonal, monthly, or hourly

How much you want to work is determined by how much money you want to make, period. The joy is that you've already got a source of income: your full-time job. Anything you make as an itinerant seller is gravy you can use to invest.

Your locations and options are limited only by your imagination and the law

You can get your products to your customers by loading up your gear in the back of your van and heading to the beach. You can set up shop outside a mall, or a bus station. You can get booth space at a craft or antiques fair. Best of all, since you don't have a huge overhead or rent to worry about, you'll be able to provide customers with better service at a lower price.

Itinerant sellers tend to bring a more personal touch to their transactions, which people like

There's more of an opportunity to get to know your customers, since there's no stock boy calling you to the back of the store or trainee tugging on your sleeve for help. It's just you and the person to whom you're trying to sell.

But there are downsides to this type of business as well. Issues you should think about include:

The work can be backbreaking
Listen, it can be a real pain in the derrière hauling around those sweaters you knit from fair to fair. As is the case with any sales job, you have to hustle to make a buck. And as with any other business, your responsibilities will include keeping track of profits, inventory, and costs, among other things.

You will have to lay out money
What, you think Santa Claus is going to bring you that hot dog cart you always dreamed of wheeling around outside Yankee Stadium? W-r-o-n-g. Fact is you're going to have to shell out for inventory (or for the materials to create your inventory, if you're a craftsperson) if you intend to have anything to sell. And as we all know—let's say this together now, class—all investment carries risk. However, if you know your product as well as the market, that risk will be minimized.

You will be at the mercy of the elements
I don't know about you, but I can't think of anything more unpleasant than standing in the freezing rain hawking roses. Not only can the weather affect your wanting to go to work, it can also eat into your profits. Who's gonna stop and buy an ice-cream cone when it's twenty-eight degrees?

Be prepared to schlep
You're itinerant, remember? That means going where the sales are, whether that means traveling from craft show to craft show selling your seashell-encrusted picture frames, or rotating your sales spot locally just to make sure you've got every base

covered. Having to travel for business means spending a lot of spare time away from home. Are you ready for that?

Is it for you?

Now that you know the pros and cons of being an itinerant seller, go back to the questions on page 215 related to starting a part-time, home-based consulting business, and ask yourself the same things. Again, honesty is crucial here. You might have a romantic image of yourself selling Victorian dried floral arrangements at craft fairs, not taking into account that you hate dealing with people! Success in sales depends on your personality. You've got to be enthusiastic and smooth enough to convince people that they need to buy what you're selling. They need to like you, and you need to be there when they need you to be, whether or not you feel like working that day.

Don't underestimate the importance creativity plays in this type of business, either. Who's going to sell more Grateful Dead T-shirts: the guy at the table with no sign or the guy playing Dead tunes on his boom box, decked out in tie-dye with a huge poster of Jerry Garcia hanging above his cart?

Whatcha gonna sell?

Fledgling writers are always told to write what they know. Well, when it comes to being a novice itinerant seller, the rule of thumb is similar: sell what you like. If you love to knit, sell sweaters, booties, scarves, hats. If you're a wonderful photographer, sell your pictures. The possibilities are endless, especially when you realize that a sizable majority of items people buy can be sold from carts, booths, or sheds. Reality-check your idea with friends, family, and coworkers by asking them what they'd buy from a vendor, or what products or services they wish they could access more conveniently. Once you've got your list down to a few items you can imagine selling, your next step is to find out:

• How often would most people who use this product want it? How often would they need to replace it?

• Can this product be purchased or produced locally?

• How convenient is it for people to get this product? Is it sold at the corner supermarket, or do they have to go out of their way to find it?

• Are people unhappy with the local store that sells this product? If so, why?

Getting started

Congratulations. You've decided to put your artistic skills to use and sell hand-painted baby furniture at craft fairs. Your process for getting started is the same as for any other business: you need to define your ideal customer and then decide whether there are enough of them in your area to support your business.

Visualize your customers—what they do, where they live, how much they earn. Now ask yourself: Where can I find them? Do you live in an area filled with young, growing families? Is the community expanding? Do your town and the surrounding areas often sponsor festivals and craft fairs where you can display your work?

Check out retailing trends. A few years back, yuppie couples would spare no expense when it came to their kids, and wouldn't think twice about paying for a darling little hand-painted rocking chair. But these days, frugality is in; they might be content to let the new baby have his big sister's old rocker. Call the U.S. Department of Commerce (301-457-4151) and get information on national retailing trends. Get a handle on which businesses are failing and which are thriving.

Having decided on your specialty, read everything you can get your hands on about it, especially trade magazines and newspapers. Remember, you need to know about the business from the retailer's perspective. Don't neglect looking at consumer magazines as well. Make sure you get in touch with relevant trade associations, as they can often be an invaluable source of information. (Contact the SBA and see if you can get a copy of the *Directory of Business, Trade, and Public Policy Organizations.*)

Next, see if you can chat with others who sell the same or similar products. The smart way to do it is to go out of town; that way you can assure people whose expertise you're milking that you're not a direct threat to them. Ask them everything you can think of about their business.

You also need to talk to potential customers to get a feeling for whether you're on the right track with the product you hope to sell. How much would your friends and acquaintances be willing to pay for such a product? Where would they be willing to go to find such a product?

Once you've canvassed everyone you know, it's time to pick the brains of the general public. Go door-to-door. Make random phone calls. Be polite and brief, presenting yourself as a neighbor rather than a salesperson. Don't take it personally if they don't want to talk to you. As was the case with part-time, home-based consulting businesses, you can run your idea past an independent observer by contacting the SBA and asking for a mentor through the SCORE program.

Those thinking of establishing a part-time, itinerant business have a few other things they need to consider. You'll have to get in touch with potential suppliers if the product you plan on selling is not one you're making yourself. Whether you're selling Tickle Me Elmo knockoffs or Peruvian sweaters, you need to be aware of the prices of these items as well as the suppliers' production schedules. If what you're selling is handcrafted but produced by others, go see the craftspeople in person. Be prepared for glitches when working with craftspeople, since their lives can be as unpredictable as yours. (All it takes is one case of little Susie getting the chicken pox or Grammy falling down the stairs and breaking her hip to bollix up even the smoothest-running production schedule.) Make sure you've got a backup supply ready.

If you're gong to be selling a retail product that's manufactured on a larger scale, contact corporate headquarters and ask to meet with the regional sales manager to discuss products and policy. Find out whether the product you want to sell is increasing or decreasing in demand, as well as what the company does to support its dealers. Don't forget that you're talking to a salesperson eager to land a new account, so he or she may be prone to exaggeration when it comes to telling you how well this product sells. To get a straight answer, ask to see the company's financial records for the past five years. If the regional salesperson refuses, walk.

The other decision unique to itinerant sellers is deciding on their sales format. Basically, you have three choices. You can:

Start a mail-order business

This is a great way to sell things you make, and it's pretty cheap to operate (not to mention handle on a part-time basis). But to be successful at it, you need interesting, eye-catching advertising. (You can even design the ads yourself if you have the right computer software). Another good way to reach customers is through cyberspace, posting ads on the Internet. Just make sure you're up on all rules and regulations when it comes to mail order. You don't want to wind up being arrested for mail fraud.

Set up a booth in a mall

Malls are high-traffic areas, which is why so many itinerant sellers do well in them. The advantages to establishing your business here is that hundreds of people will pass by your booth daily. The disadvantage is that you might have to pay a pretty penny for the space you occupy, even if it's a little out-of-the-way. In all honesty, mall work will probably not pay for itself if you're going to be doing this on a part-time basis.

Sell from a peddler's cart

Walk down any city street and you'll see them: vendors with carts selling everything from tofu burgers to perfume. You will need a license to operate such a cart, and competition for prime, high-traffic areas can be fierce. Check with city hall or the local chamber of commerce. Also keep in mind that you'll be at the mercy of the elements.

For more information on starting an itinerant business, check out the following books:

- *How to Open Your Own Store,* by Michael Antoniak (Avon Books, 1994).
- *How to Start a Mail Order Business for under $10,000,* by Mike Powers (Avon Books, 1996).
- *How to Start a Retirement Business,* by Jacqueline Powers (Avon Books, 1996).
- *From Dogs to Riches: A Step-by-Step Guide to Start and Operate Your Own Mobile Cart Vending Business,* by Vera D. Clark-Rugley (MCC Publishing, 1993).
- *Start and Run a Profitable Craft Business: Your Step-by-Step Business Plan,* by William Hynes (Self-Counsel Press, 1993).
- *Selling What You Make: Profit from Your Handcrafts,* by James E. Seitz (McGraw-Hill, 1992).
- *Starting a Business to Sell Your Craft Items* (Business of Your Own, 1988).
- *Starting a Business to Sell Your Artwork* (Business of Your Own, 1988).
- *Start Your Own Gift Basket Business,* edited by JoAnn Padgett (Pfeiffer, 1994).

Mobile service business

A mobile service business is one in which you sell your effort, expertise, and time, rather than a specific product. House-cleaning and lawn maintenance services are two good examples of mobile service businesses. The key is that the service is brought directly to your client, making the business easier to start, not to mention less expensive. Why? Because you don't have to worry about paying rent. You can run your business out of your home, or take it to the streets via the trunk of your car.

The mobile service business is booming, and understandably so. As people find themselves with less and less leisure time, they're more willing to pay others to do the things they no longer have the time or inclination to tackle. That's where you come in.

The opportunities for a mobile service business are endless. People are looking to hire others to do everything from walking their dogs to polishing their furniture to cleaning their pool. In fact, it's estimated that come the 21st century, close to 90 percent of all jobs will be service-based. Not only are more and more people too busy to spend their free time tackling mundane tasks, there also more and more people in the position of having enough money to pay others to do things for them.

In addition, people are living longer. Show me an octogenarian who's out there mowing his own lawn in the ninety-degree heat and I'll show you a lunatic with a death wish or a prime customer for a mobile service business. Difficult as it might be to think about, the older we get, the less we're able to do, especially when it comes to physical activities. What does this mean for you? Profit. Because anything someone can't do, or won't do, has the potential to become a mobile service business.

Let me start by listing the pros of this kind of business:

You don't need to be a brain surgeon to start this type of business

What you do need is the willingness to bust your butt, as well as the willingness to do a job—any job—that others would gladly pay for.

You don't need a lot of money to get started

In many cases it will cost you next to nothing to get the business launched. For instance, all you need to become a housecleaner is cleaning supplies.

You can work as much or as little as you'd like

If you want more clients, you can solicit new business, but if you're happy with two regular customers, just keep them happy and forget about further advertising or marketing.

Before you start printing your business cards, you need to know about the downsides to this type of business as well:

You're often at the mercy of the elements

You can't clean a pool, wash a window, or rake a leaf in a torrential downpour. If the business you're considering is based on being outdoors, be aware that even the best-laid plans can be sidetracked by the weather.

People can be unpredictable

What do you do if you've got your schedule for the week all figured out, and one of your clients calls to switch the day or time? While in most cases you will be able to accommodate your client, having to juggle your carefully laid plans around is likely to throw you off. So be aware that this kind of stress goes with the territory.

It's damn hard work

The vast majority of mobile service businesses require physical labor. Ask yourself: Am I really up to running errands for two hours every evening after working all day? You need to realistically assess how much energy you have, and how much of that energy will be available to put into a service business venture.

You won't wind up as rich as Bill Gates

Can you make money? Yes, but not heaps, especially if you're only going to be doing this part-time.

IS A MOBILE SERVICE BUSINESS IN YOUR FUTURE?

It could be. But you won't know until you do some honest soul-searching, and then take another look at the list of what it takes to be a successful entrepreneur on page 214. The first thing you need to grapple with is whether you're willing to invest the money to get the business off the ground. Granted, the start-up cost is minimal, but there's no point in pouring your hard-earned cash into a venture you might not have thought through.

Next, think about your personality. Are you flexible, patient, hardworking? Are you willing to live by the old adage that the customer is always right? Are you humble? After all, much of what you'll be doing could be considered "menial" labor. If that bothers you, forget mobile service businesses. If you know that who you are has nothing to do with what you're doing to pick up extra money, this might be the right type of business for you.

While it helps to have skill or expertise in the business you're offering, it's not a hard-and-fast requirement. What's more important is that you're willing to do what it takes to succeed. The truth is, most mobile service jobs are not intellectually stimulating or the least bit challenging. They tend to be jobs that are incredibly repetitive, incredibly simple, and not very creative. So if you're someone who needs to be challenged constantly or has the attention span of a four-year-old, don't even think of starting a mobile service business.

WHAT KIND OF SERVICE SHOULD YOU PROVIDE?

The type of service you provide will depend on how much time you have, your personality, and the local need for the service. Most mobile service jobs fall into the following broad categories:

Servicing lifestyle needs

This can be anything from helping a harried mother plan and throw her son's birthday party to redecorating homes. The key to success is pinpointing the lifestyle of a particular demographic group and figuring out what services would save them time and enhance their way of living.

Repairing stuff

The acceptance of planned obsolence seems to be waning. Today, more and more people are opting to have equipment and goods repaired rather than rushing out to replace them at the first sign of wear. This includes every type of product you can think of, from food processors to Dustbusters.

Doing household chores

I don't know about you, but the last thing I want to do is clean the house or maintain the yard after a day of working. Most people feel the same way—which is why the demand for housecleaning services continues to rise.

Filling gaps in business support services

Before corporate downsizing, many large businesses boasted a cleaning staff, a cafeteria staff, and mail room staff. No more. Now these jobs are often being filled by those in the mobile service industry who'll come in, do a job, and spare the business owner the expense of having to pay benefits.

Filling staff gaps

You've heard how temps are taking over the workplace? Well, that's what this is all about. More and more businesses are turning to outside workers to do everything from bookkeeping to PR (again, it saves them money on benefits). As a temp, you can determine how few or how many hours you want to work, whether you want a long-term gig or one that lasts just a few weeks, even how far you're willing to travel to work.

THE NEED FOR BIFOCAL VISION

The successful mobile business owner doesn't only have an eye on the services required today. He or she is also aware of emerging trends—trends that could result in a new opportunities for business. To make sure you're on top of future possibilities, try the following:

Park your butt on the couch and watch TV

I'm not talking about your weekly turn-off-the-phone, turn-down-the-lights ritual of watching *The X-Files.* I'm talking about channel surfing at all different hours of the day and night, so you get a feel for what other people might watch or buy. For example, shows dealing with the supernatural are hot right now, meaning that anything from angel key chains to T-shirts reading "I Believe" could potentially sell if marketed correctly.

Read lots of different specialty magazines and newspapers

I'm talking ethnic publications, hobby publications—anything that can provide you with insights into a particular niche of people. Once you're aware of what type of people constitute a particular demographic group, you should be able to come up with ideas for services you can provide them with. For example, let's say you notice that country decor seems to be popular in many of the home decorating magazines, and you just happen to sew handmade quilts. There's nothing to stop you from placing an ad in one of these magazines to sell your wares, or finding out when and where the biggest craft sales in your area take place.

As is the case with any business you're launching on your own, assess:

- Whether this service is available locally.
- If so, is it convenient to clients? Is it expensive or cheap?
- How often a client would use this service—daily? weekly? monthly? seasonally?
- Have you ever hired someone to perform this service for you? How much were you willing to pay? What pleased or displeased you about using the service?

GETTING STARTED

Based on your answers to the questions above, you should have a pretty good idea as to whether there's a need in your area for the service you want to provide.

Just as you were advised in the sections on starting a home-based or an itinerant selling business, define your ideal client, then determine whether there are enough of them in your area to support your business. Remember, you're bringing the service to them, which means you'd like them to be in as close proximity to you as possible. In addition, you need to figure out how and where you can reach these clients, since all future marketing efforts will be directed at where these clients can be found.

Once you've got a detailed image of your clients in your head—complete with where they shop and live, what they earn, and what kinds of other services they are likely to be interested in—you need to locate them. Are most of them found in the nearby condo complex for the aging? In the city? In the suburbs?

Your next move should be talking to other people in the field. Again, the trick to getting the skinny might be to go outside the community you live in and interview people who won't see you as direct competition. Ask all the same questions advised in the other two sections, such as whether or not their business is thriving, what clients like and dislike, and whether there are any business do's and don'ts.

Once you've got a rough idea of what it's like to run this kind of business from someone who knows the ropes, it's time to run your idea by potential clients. Again: talk to friends, family, and neighbors. Make phone calls. Knock on doors. And definitely, definitely contact the SBA about the SCORE program.

For more information on starting a part-time mobile service business, you might want to peruse the following books:

- *Catering: Start and Run a Money-Making Business,* by Judy Richards (McGraw-Hill, 1994).
- *Starting and Operating a Landscape Maintenance Business,* by Laurence Price (Botany Books, 1980).
- *How to Start a Service Business,* by Ben Chant and Melissa Morgan (Avon Books, 1994).
- *How to Start and Operate a Recycling Business,* by John P. Allison (RMC Publishing Group, 1991).
- *Painting Contractor: Start and Run a Money-Making Business,* by Dan Ramsey (TAB Books, 1993).
- *How to Start a Window Cleaning Business: A Guide to Sales, Procedures, and Operations,* by Judy Suvall (Cleaning Consultants, 1988).

GETTING A NEW FULL-TIME JOB

Most people find the prospect of looking for another job even more frightening than asking for a raise or starting a business. And just as there's no such thing as job security, it's true that seniority and experience don't count for a whole lot these days.

But that doesn't mean finding a new, higher-paying job is impossible. Despite the fact that large companies will continue to treat employees as if they're merely costs to be slashed, the same isn't true when it comes to new and expanding businesses. On the contrary, small and medium-sized businesses, new companies, and foreign companies are all doing more hiring than firing. Strut the right stuff, and you could find yourself newly employed at such a company.

But first, you've got to realize that the workplace of today is slowly morphing into something new, requiring workers' acceptance of different kinds of benefits, work skills, and work situations. In preparing to launch a job hunt, be aware that you:

• Will probably be required to work as part of a team, rather than as part of a department. This isn't just semantics; the change in wording reflects a new flexibility on the part of employees—a flexibility they expect you to share.

• Might not have your own office . . . and might not even have an office at all. As I mentioned earlier, more and more people are working out of their homes. Many are self-employed, but those who aren't are known as telecommuters. You could be one.

• Probably won't have a support staff. Not only will you have to go get your own coffee, you'll be doing your own scheduling, answering your own telephone, and handling your own correspondence, all with your PC, software, printer, and modem. In fact, you'll probably be doing all the functions needed to support your major task.

In addition to the possibility (that is, the probability) of finding yourself in a reconstituted work situation, chances are you're also going to have to be open to new kinds of compensation and benefits. Gone are the days of fully funded pension plans and comprehensive health coverage, as well as pay based on experience and seniority. Instead, today's employer offers:

• Experience-enhancing opportunities, as well as the chance to achieve success in a number of different areas.

• Education and training that will broaden your skills.

• Pay based on adaptability, flexibility, knowledge, skill, and, most important of all, results, rather than seniority or longevity.

All these changes stem from the fact that the traditional relationship between employers and employees is as dead as Marley's ghost. In its place has emerged a new "contract," one based not on the conventional hierarchical structure of the workplace, but rather on the notion that employers and employees are partners. According to the new terms of the workplace, employers:

- Recognize employee contributions to the company;
- Actively seek out employee participation;
- Offer fair play and adequate benefits, based on how well the employee performs for the company;
- Provide opportunities for growth;
- Provide a safe, healthy, worker-friendly environment;
- Provide free and open access to information.

In return, today's employees:

- Work their tails off for the company;
- Behave ethically and honestly;
- Demonstrate commitment to the company's goals;
- Offer suggestions that might improve the running or profitability of the company;
- Are willing to undertake training that will improve their productivity.

In addition, both employers and employees agree that together, their focus should be on satisfying customer needs and desires.

Job-hunting tips

Now that you're aware that it's a new kind of jungle out there, you need to get in gear and begin the process of looking for a job. Below, a few tips to help you get started.

Think of yourself as a commodity

In order to sell yourself to an employer, you have to know what your strengths are, how it would benefit him or her to have you as part of the company, and what unique skills and experiences you have to offer. Think of yourself, then, as a product to be sold.

Mum's the word when it comes to your job search

The fewer people at your current place of business who know you're looking for a new job, the better. Obviously, it's impossible to keep it completely under your chapeau—after all, the people you're contacting for a job will know. But beyond them and your immediate family, that should be it. The reason? If God forbid your boss finds out you're looking to light out for greener pastures, your name will be Mudd. Not only will you be his number one candidate come layoff time, but you'll also find yourself left out of all important meetings. Worst of all, you'll be viewed as a traitor.

Do whatever you can to keep your company in the dark about your job search. To do so:

• Don't wear a suit to work if you usually dress as if every day is dress-down Friday.
• Avoid taking too many sick days.
• Make sure you don't start a pattern of coming in late or leaving early.
• Try to schedule job interviews during your lunch hour. If that's impossible, see if they can be held before or after working hours. If you have to take time off for an interview, take the whole day and try to maximize your time, arranging for an interview in the morning and one in the afternoon.
• Keep office phone calls to a minimum.
• If you can, arrange to have all job-search correspondence sent to your home.

Network, network, network

Here's a factoid you might want to know: Close to 70 percent of all job openings are filled through personal contacts. This means you should be out yakking it up with everyone you know, soliciting both guidance and advice. How does that jibe with keeping your job search a secret? Well, the solution is to keep your mouth shut around coworkers, but to be gregarious about your search away from the office. Call all your outside business and personal contacts and tell them you're looking for a new job. (Make sure you add that this is not news to be broadcast.) Tell them you're hoping they might be able to give

236 • Investing for Retirement

you some guidance and advice, and that you're open to meeting with anyone they can think of to discuss possibilities.

This might seem like a scattershot approach, but it really isn't. Rather, think of it as throwing a stone in the water. What happens to the surface of the water when the stone hits? It forms ripples. Networking does the same thing. While the person you speak with might not know of a job, he may know of someone who knows someone who knows someone. . . .

Most people don't mind helping out in this way, either. One of the great unwritten rules of business is "What goes around, comes around." This means that if I help you, one day you'll be willing to do the same for me, and so on. It's good karma.

Forget about headhunters, want ads, bulk mailings, and employment agencies

Headhunters are generally paid by specific companies to fill specific positions. The same goes for employment agencies. Half the time they don't even bother to call when a position comes available. The other half of the time they call to let you know about a job that pays next to nothing. Avoid them both.

As for answering want ads, be aware that hundreds, if not thousands, of work-hungry people may be answering the same ad you're answering. Similarly, there are thousands of people out there blindly sending their résumés to the same companies you are. Their chances of getting a job are mighty slim—as are yours.

Go on line to look for work

Here's a list of some sites on the World Wide Web that function as huge help wanted bulletin boards. Definitely worth a look are:

• JobWeb (http://www.jobweb.org). Listings are indexed by profession and region. Links are provided to resources such as professional associations.

• Career Links (http://www.careertalk.com/career–links.html). This links you to other career-related sites on the Web.

• Job Search and Employment Opportunities: Best Bets from the Net (http://asa.ugl.lib.umich.edu/chdocs/employment/job-guide.toc.html). This list, managed by the University of Michigan's library, lists nationwide job openings by category and occupation.

• Career Mosaic (http://www.careermosaic.com). Lets you search thousands of postings on the JOBS database and in Usenet newsgroups via topic or keyword.

• Online Career Center (http://www.occ.com/occ). A job database searchable by industry, state, and city.

• E-span (http://www.espan.com). Imagine 10,000 paid help wanted ads you can scan for free! That's E-span. In addition to being able to key in your own résumé summary and use various keywords to help you track down possible matches, you can also arrange to have potential leads sent to you via e-mail.

• Monster Board (http://www.monster.com). The mother of all job databases on the Net, boasting roughly 50,000 listings that can be searched by title, region, or industry. You can also submit your own résumé to a database that's searched by employers, as well as check out a calendar of nationwide job fairs.

Putting together a killer résumé

Your résumé should be put together with one goal in mind: to get you an interview. In order to do that, though, your résumé not only has to maximize what you've accomplished, it also has to minimize potential negatives. If it doesn't achieve that, you'll never get that first foot in the door.

I know that sounds awfully pessimistic, perhaps even fatalistic, but it's true. Most résumés are used by employers as negative screening devices to narrow the search for a job candidate. Upon receiving a résumé, the first thing a suit does is scan it for lack of expertise and experience so he or she can immediately disqualify that candidate. That's not so bad. But after that, the process gets subjective. Some executives have been known to

eliminate candidates based on where they earned their degree—
"She went to Yale? Forget it. I'll only interview Harvard
women"—or what company they work for. Others throw out
the résumés of those who have stuck with one company for a
long time, or, conversely, those who have job-hopped too often.
Sound unfair? It is. But the primary concern for the first person
screening résumés is to cut down the number of potential inter-
viewees to a manageable count.

Since you'd like to be one of the chosen few who make the
final cut, it's absolutely crucial your résumé stresses achievements and skills rather than your career chronology, since it's
chronology that's most likely to be your downfall.

The achievements you cite should zero in on one thing: how
you helped increase the profits of the companies you've worked
for, either by boosting revenues or helping contain or cut costs.
This means going into great detail about your accomplishments
and translating them into dollars and cents.

Think about every professional job you've worked, and try
to come up with examples where your efforts helped make the
company money. Be as specific as you can. It'll help if you
can come up with dollar amounts, but if you can't, just give a
rough estimate. Avoid the temptation to inflate the figure—"I
helped the company save three million dollars!"

Unfortunately, putting together an achievement-oriented résumé doesn't mean you can forget about giving potential employers your career chronology. All suits want to know where
you've worked and for how long. The trick is including the
chronology after you've listed your achievements, so they read
up on the positives first before getting to potential negatives.

Keep in mind also that how you format your chronology can
have a big impact upon whether you're perceived negatively or
positively. To minimize the feeling of job-hopping show that
each career move has meant an increase in responsibility and
salary. Explain away gaps in the chronology by detailing how
that time was used—for example, perhaps you went back to
school to update your skills. If you've been with one company

since the dawn of time, list every promotion, salary increase, and change in responsibility as a separate entry. This will show progression.

Many people are tempted to do away with the section at the end of a résumé where you list your interests. After all, you think, what does the employer care that you do tai chi or were named Racquetball King of Bergen County? The fact is, listing interests can help you. Let's say you do tai chi. The employer might surmise, then, that you're someone who's learned how to handle stress. Similarly, being the racquetball king shows you're fit and healthy—something an employer looks for but can't ask about.

The more specific you are about your interests, the more interesting you appear to be. You never know—the employer could have been named Racquetball King of Monmouth County, in which case you'll be hired on the spot and will also have a partner with whom to play the game during lunch.

One final word about résumés: Avoid glitz, glamour, and gimmicks. You may think it will help your cause to print your résumé on shocking blue paper, or write it up in Middle English, but it won't. If anything, it will alienate potential employers, as they'll perceive you as someone with no respect for business norms. Boring as it might sound, try to keep your résumé to two pages or less, and stick with ten-to-twelve-point serif typefaces printed in black on white paper.

Acing the interview

Let's assume you're one of the lucky few who make it to the interview stage. Now is not the time to rest on your laurels hoping your résumé will make your case for you. It's time to get revved up, because it's how you perform during your interview that will land you the job.

Your physical appearance has got to be impeccable. But just as important, you've got to come across as well prepared. This means walking into the interview knowing as much as you can about the interviewer as well as the company.

If you've managed to get the interview as a result of net-working, pump the intermediary for all he or she knows about the person you'll be speaking with. Next, go online or to the library and dig up all you can about the company. Scan newspapers, trade journals, and magazines to ascertain all you can about where the company is placed within the industry. While all the information you glean might not come up within the context of the interview, it's good to know nonetheless, if only for the fact that it's likely to make you feel more confident and relaxed, and that will help you create a better impression.

Perhaps it's been a while since you've been on a job interview. Below are the questions most often asked by interviewers. The more completely you're able to answer them, the better your chances of success.

- Why do you want to work here?
- Why do you think you're qualified for this job?
- Why are you looking for a job?
- Why did you leave your last job?
- What are your strengths?
- What are your weaknesses?
- What are your personal goals?
- What are your career goals?
- What did you like and dislike about your previous jobs?
- Where do you see yourself in five years?
- What are your greatest professional achievements?
- What are your greatest personal achievements?
- How would you characterize your work and management styles?
- Have you ever had to deal with a difficult boss or subordinate?

Don't feel you have to walk into the interview with a canned answer for every one of these questions. It's more important that you appear comfortable answering them. Be concise and do whatever you can to stress the positive. You must, however, also be prepared to address the negatives. Your goal is to come across as polished and professional.

To this end, you should come to the interview prepared to ask some questions of your own. Failure to do so will brand you as uninterested or, worse, passive. The questions below will not only help you glean valuable info about the company you could end up working for, but will also make you sound like you've got lots o' smarts.

- What are the major responsibilities of this position?
- What opportunities for advancement are there in this company?
- What happened to the person who previously held this position?
- Whom does the person in this position report to?
- What's the work atmosphere like in this company?
- How much support staff will be available?
- What would you consider to be the drawbacks of this position?
- Has the budget for this department been increasing or decreasing?
- Where do you see the company going in the next five years?

It's important you do research right up until the day of the interview, including reading that day's paper, just in case the interviewer brings up a story in the news and asks you for your opinion on how it might affect the industry.

If the interview lands you the job, congratulations. But if it doesn't, don't let it demoralize you. Instead, turn a negative into a positive by contacting the interviewer and asking for help. Say you're interested in improving your interpersonal skills, and you would find it beneficial if she or he could point out to you any weaknesses in your presentation. This is a good way to get an unbiased critique that can help you do a better job next time around.

Negotiating salary

You might think that once you're offered a new job, the process of job-hunting is through. It isn't. Landing a new job is actually a two-part process: first you've got to convince the employer he wants to hire you, then you've got to convince him to pay you what you're worth. After all, you're making this move in order to come up with the added money you need to invest for your retirement. Your success at coming up with enough money to fund your retirement program is contingent on your negotiating salary before you accept a job.

Your starting salary in a new job is the single most important factor that will determine whether you'll be generating enough income to invest for retirement. As you know from your own experience as well as from reading this book, raises are tough to come by and are often tied to your starting salary. That's why it's crucial to come out of the starting gate earning good money.

Most employers have a salary range in mind for a particular position. If it's a newly created job, chances are there's a specific figure budgeted for salary. If it's a job that's just been vacated, the company is probably looking to pay you less than the last person who held the job—although if pressed, they might be willing to pay more if they think you'll contribute more to the company.

To maximize your chances of landing the salary you want, follow these three simple rules: Never accept a job immediately, realize there are things other than money involved, and don't be the first to spit out a dollar figure.

If the interviewer mentions salary first, it means he wants you for the job. But it also means you can negotiate the number up. That wouldn't be the case if you spit out a number first. Some employers are wily and will try to get you to name a number first by asking questions like "How much of a salary are you looking for?" If that happens, throw the ball back in their court by responding, "I'm looking for a salary commensurate with my skills and experience. What salary are you willing to pay the person who takes this position?"

Of course, you could find yourself going back and forth, with neither of you willing to name a dollar figure. If push comes to shove, name a figure. Just make sure it's high enough for you to be able to negotiate down and still walk away with a salary higher than the one you're currently pulling in today.

You can assume there's going to be some degree of flexibility—usually 20 to 25 percent—about salary. Naturally the employer is going to offer you a figure at the low end of the range, so feel free to counter with a salary from the top end of the range, say 10 to 20 percent higher.

No matter what figures get bandied about, don't accept a salary offer immediately, even if it is a good one. Instead, look the interviewer directly in the eye and ask, "Is that the best you can do?" Keep looking at him until he gives you an answer. And no matter what that answer is, tell him you're excited about the position but you'd like to go home, think about things, and get back to them the next morning. Don't be surprised if he offers you a higher figure right on the spot to close the deal, rather than risking your possibly turning down the job.

Keep in mind when negotiating salary that there's more to being compensated than the dollar figure on your pay stub every week. Compensation can include things like medical coverage, tuition reimbursement, and a title, in addition to salary. Include them in your negotiations. Just make sure you don't agree to take any compensation that doesn't directly translate into more dollars in your pocket. After all, that was the whole point of getting a new job.

ALL ABOARD THE REALITY TRAIN

So here we are. You know where you're starting from and where you want to end up in retirement. You know all about the different tools and techniques to help you get there. And now, with this chapter and the one before, you know of a number of different ways to trim expenses and boost revenues in order to generate enough money to invest for retirement.

But what if it doesn't all add up? What if there's no feasible way you can retire the way you want, no matter how ruthlessly you cut expenses or how diligently you toil to boost your income? Must you abandon your retirement dreams completely?

The answer, you'll be happy to know, is no. All you've got to do is go back to the drawing board and draw yourself a new picture of retirement. With a few minor changes here and there, you can still retire in a manner close to your original vision. To find how, turn the page.

17

BACK TO THE DRAWING BOARD

As you've discovered from reading this book, successfully investing for retirement is contingent on setting clear-cut goals and creating an individually plotted road map to achieve them. But what if, after all is said and done, it doesn't look like you're going to be able to fund the retirement of your dreams? Should you just forget about the whole thing and do what most people do, which is stick their head in the sand and pray for the best?

Absolutely not.

It's not uncommon for people to go through the process of planning for retirement only to find that, in the end, there's no way they're going to be able to retire in the manner they've dreamed of, within the time frame they've set for themselves. There are a number of reasons for this.

Chances are your vision of retirement features every single perk and leisure activity you can imagine. You've left no fantasy untapped. The life you see for yourself is top-of-the-line with nary a compromise in sight.

Or your dreams may be based on when you want to retire, as well as an investment strategy that reflects your long-held views about financial risk, whatever they may be.

Finally, you may have based your desires on a superficial assessment of how much sacrifice you're willing to make in terms of spending as well as of reducing expenses.

But now that it's become clear that you can't achieve your vision of retirement as it stands, something has to give. You've got to be willing to change a piece of the puzzle—maybe even more than one—to make everything fit. Why? Because if you don't, you won't even come close to ending up with what you want. Painful as it may be to think about, you're going to have to make some compromises. But where?

Start by going back to the beginning and reevaluating the elements that helped you figure out how to get from where you are to where you want to be: location, work, timing, risk, expenses, and revenue. Examining them one by one, you might be able to come up with some compromises that can help you remain true to your original vision, or at the very least close to it.

LOCATION

Perhaps your dream vision of retirement entails moving away. But if it's going to adversely affect your quality of life, you might want to explore the option of staying put. Conversely, maybe you imagined staying right where you are, in the same house and town. But if it's not possible, you might need to think about moving to a smaller living space, or to another town—or part of the country—entirely. This is what Chuck and Nora McGinty have realized they need to do.

As you'll recall, Chuck wanted to retire in five years, and Nora wanted to remain in their home on Long Island. But after working through the numbers, they now see that the high cost of living on Long Island will dramatically affect how far their money will go. Rather than both working, taking out a reverse mortgage, and still living hand to mouth just so Nora can stay in the house she proudly decorated, they've decided that when Chuck retires, they will move down to South Carolina, where the cost of living is much lower. They'll be close to their daughter in Atlanta, and best of all, they'll be able to maintain the quality of life to which they've grown accustomed.

WORK

If you're like many people, going through the process of planning for retirement has revealed to you that you might not be able to retire fully as you'd hoped. So you need to ask yourself: If I continue to work part-time in retirement, will I be able to at least achieve the rest of my retirement dream? Will it allow me to stay where I am, if that's what I want? Or retire on the timetable I've set for myself? If so, it might be an option worth exploring, especially if it means not having to compromise your retirement dreams in any other way.

TIMING

How compatible is your timetable for retirement with your retirement dreams? If the answer is "not very," consider extending the time line and working for longer than you previously envisioned.

This is what Tim Harper has decided to do. Tim, as you know, had visions of early retirement dancing in his head. But after it became abundantly clear to him and wife Sarah that this option was out, (especially if they wanted to remain on the East Coast and reside in the rural but pricey town of Bennington when they retired), Tim decided that the compromise he'd be willing to make to keep the rest of his retirement vision intact would be to work for five to ten years longer.

If the thought of working longer doesn't exactly float your boat, consider this: The longer you work, the more time your money has to grow. In addition, the amount you'll ultimately receive from Social Security will be higher.

RISK

Take a look at the kinds of investments you envision making to help fund your retirement, and the amount of risk involved. If all your investments are on the conservative side and you find you're coming up short, you might want to consider taking a bit more of a risk with some of your money, especially if such a move is coupled with working even longer than expected (the reason for this being you'll be better able to recoup any losses you might incur). Believe it or not, a small adjustment like this can be the key to getting the most out of all your investments.

EXPENSES AND REVENUE

Now that you've determined that with things as they stand, you won't be able to get what you want in retirement, ask yourself: Is it worth it for me to cut back now so I can have the lifestyle I want later? Or: Am I willing to break my back now bringing in more money so I can achieve my goals for retirement? If so, go back over the last two chapters and see what you can do to trim expenses and increase your revenues. This is what Mitch and Sheryl Kahn are doing.

Not wanting to alter the timetable they've set up for retirement, and determined to retire to Florida, they've started slashing expenses: Sheryl now does her own nails rather than handing over $30 per month to the manicurist, and Mitch, an avid reader, has decided to get a library card rather than buy the books he wants to read. In addition, Mitch has started doing some sales consulting work on the side. By making these small adjustments, and keeping their eyes on the prize, the Kahns should have less trouble fulfilling the vision of retirement they originally created for themselves.

Hopefully, making minor modifications in just one of the above areas will help you achieve the retirement of your dreams. But if compromising in one area isn't sufficient, look to rethinking your goals in another area—or however many areas it takes for you to come up with an image of your retirement you can live with and achieve.

WORKING WITH WHAT YOU'VE GOT

I don't know about you, but the first time I did all the exercises in this book and realized I was going to have to adjust my vision of retirement, I felt like a complete and utter failure. What else could explain why I was falling short of the mark?

If you're feeling the same way, you need to realize that you're only falling short of an unrealistic mark you have set for yourself. Too often, people look at their friends, relatives, and coworkers and feel they themselves "don't measure up." What I want to know is: measure up to what? The income, dreams, and life circumstances of every individual are different. So what if your cousin Tommy makes half a million a year and will be able to retire at age 40? You can't live Tommy's life, and he can't live yours. What is the point, then, of comparing yourself to him—or indeed to anyone?

Perhaps you're looking at the previous generation and thinking, you're a failure because you won't be able to retire fully to Florida and spend your days thinking up ways to make your adult children feel guilty about not visiting you. In that case, allow me to refresh your memory: Members of the previous generation were in a unique situation when it came to retirement. Not only was there enough money in the system for them in the form of company pensions, Social Security, and other federal aid, but they were also able to take advantage of an inflated real estate market, the likes of which this country will probably never see again. Those retiring today or in the future aren't likely to have any of those factors working for them in retirement, at least not the way things look now. So stop feeling like a total loser because your retirement ain't gonna be as "golden" as dear old Dad's. Dear old Dad got lucky.

It all boils down to this: All you can do is do your best with whatever tools are at your disposal. That's it. If you work a forklift and know that's going to be your job for the next thirty years, then dammit, you should be the best forklift operator there is and do what you can within the parameters of your own life circumstances. But do not beat yourself up because your annual earnings are never going to rival Oprah's.

Instead, focus on the road before you, coming to terms with where you need and want to go. At the end of the road, you want to be able to look back at whatever it was you did and feel proud. So maybe Chuck and Nora McGinty aren't going to be able to stay on Long Island as they'd planned. But they were able to put all their kids through college, and knowing they accomplished that makes adjusting their retirement plans a little easier.

All life is compromise. Figure out what you can do, and make that your retirement dream. Just make sure you set aside time to enjoy yourself along the way. Because when all is said and done, it's the journey that matters.

INDEX

BUILD YOUR OWN BUSINESS LIBRARY

with the

21ST CENTURY ENTREPRENEUR SERIES!

HOW TO OPEN A FRANCHISE BUSINESS
Mike Powers   77912-9/$12.50 US/$16.00 Can

HOW TO OPEN YOUR OWN STORE
Michael Antoniak   77076-8/$12.50 US/$15.00 Can

HOW TO START A HOME BUSINESS
Michael Antoniak   77911-0/$12.50 US/$16.00 Can

HOW TO START A SERVICE BUSINESS
Ben Chant and Melissa Morgan
                                 77077-6/$12.50 US/$15.00 Can

HOW TO START A MAIL ORDER BUSINESS
Mike Powers   78446-7/$12.50 US/$16.50 Can

HOW TO START A RETIREMENT BUSINESS
Jacqueline K. Powers   78447-5/$12.50 US/$16.50 Can